UNDRESSING

UNDRESSING

by James O'Neill

with a foreword by Adam Phillips

Published in 2019 by Short Books,
Unit 316, ScreenWorks,
22 Highbury Grove,
London, N5 2ER

10 9 8 7 6 5 4 3 2 1

Copyright © 2019 James O'Neill

Foreword copyright © 2019 Adam Phillips

A CIP catalogue record for this book is
available from the British Library.

ISBN: 978-1-78072-394-5

Cover design by Chris Bentham

Printed at CPI Group (UK) Ltd, Croydon, CR0 4YY

For A.M. (as promised)

Contents

Contents

Foreword

WHEN FREUD WORRIED, EARLY ON IN his career, that his case histories sounded rather like "short stories", or even "novellas", he was alerting us to the fact that his new science of psychoanalysis was about what art was about. That psychoanalysis – just like Sophocles's *Oedipus Rex*, or *Hamlet*, or Goethe's *Faust*, or *Don Quixote*, or the more contemporary novels that Freud also admired, and treated as his precursors – was about nothing more and nothing less than people's difficulties in living. That the material of psychoanalysis was the material of great, and not so great, art (psychoanalysis should be of interest to people who are not interested in psychoanalysis). That psychoanalysis was part of a larger and longer cultural conversation – partly religious, partly political, partly artistic – about how and why to live. About what might matter most to us, and about whether what does matter most is sufficiently

11

sustaining. And this, indeed, is what O'Neill's extraordinary book is about.

It has taken a lot of work – work that psychoanalysts have done all too eagerly – to make the writing of psychoanalysis as dull or as unengaging as it so often is, given what the therapist experiences, day in, day out, in their practice. As though when people write about psychoanalysis they lose heart, or humour, or appeal. You would never guess, reading the psychoanalytic literature, that the most moving, poignant, intriguing and amusing conversations were being described. This book, among so many other things, sets the record straight. The singularity of the so-called patient is never lost in misleading generalisations of theory, and theory is used sparingly and to the point.

In O'Neill's book – at once a case-history, a novella, and something more than either – we have a remarkable story of what two people can do for each other if they can experiment with trust; neither wishfully taking it for granted, nor despairingly assuming its impossibility (to experiment with trust is to experiment with knowingness). Indeed, it is part of the ingenuity of this book that O'Neill can write so inspiringly about something as hackneyed as trust, and without sentimental compromise.

With none of the virtuous worthiness or virtuous rigour that mars therapy writing, O'Neill writes about two people, drawn to each other for different reasons, as is usually the case, discovering what they can do with each other – what can be possible between them – when coercion is not the name of the game. And the book makes very clear that the nature of the contract in therapy – one person offering help to another – has tended to obscure the quality of the relationship and its mutuality. There is always the far-reaching significance of who each member of the couple happens to be (as O'Neill intimates, the patient walks straight into the analyst's personal history). It is one of the marvels of this book that O'Neill shows us what it might be – as a therapist, but not only as a therapist – to be present without being purposeful.

O'Neill's sensibility – in the plain and subtle art-fulness of his sentences – is startling in its sympathetic intelligence, in his tact and his straightforwardness. And in his showing Abraham – the aptly named patient – as not a new kind of hero, but as something better; as someone working out how to be a new kind of man from such devastated beginnings.

Adam Phillips, July 2018

Chapter One

On Meeting Abraham

"To restore the human subject at the centre – the
suffering, afflicted, fighting, human subject, we must
deepen the case history to a narrative or tale."
Oliver Sacks, *The Man Who Mistook*
His Wife For a Hat, 1985

I FIRST MET ABRAHAM ON A very hot summer's day
some thirty years ago. At the time we'd agreed on
the phone, I went down to reception but there were
only two middle-aged women waiting there. I sat and
waited with them. I was anxious and felt unprepared,
fearing equally that he wouldn't turn up and that he
would. After about ten minutes of this fretting, a young
black man walked into the room and sat down. He was

dressed in a green anorak, zipped tightly and with the hood up. The three of us watched him suspiciously. He didn't look up; his gaze was locked onto an invisible spot on the floor. But this had to be him – and he did look rather disturbed. I stood up, went over to him and asked if he was Abraham. He nodded. I introduced myself and told him to follow me upstairs to a room where we could talk. Once inside, I indicated a chair and he sat down, without removing his coat, gloves, hat or scarf, and again stared at the floor. Thus far we'd not made eye contact and he hadn't uttered a word.

I had just started a placement at a therapy centre situated in the grounds of a Catholic convent in West London. I had yet to be referred any patients as the first year of my training was devoted solely to theory, but now I was keen to get into the consulting room, to get going with the work itself. My supervisor Agnes was a bright and warm Swiss woman in her late sixties, who described herself as a "liberated Jungian". Freed up from dogma and theoretical certainty by age and experience, she was willing to take risks, to act on her instincts, and during one of our early meetings she asked me if I would see a young man who had come seeking therapy several months back. The notes made of his interview suggested that he might be psychotic and therefore traditionally considered unsuitable for talking therapy. His referral form had subsequently languished in a discarded pile in the basement. Agnes had come upon it there. She told me she had a hunch that we might hit it off. She said that there is always a danger that people of different cultures are wrongly diagnosed and that all too often trauma, alienation and loneliness are misunderstood as symptoms of psychosis. She suggested I give it a go and see how I got on, see if he'd open up with me. She told me that I'd need to be very patient just to get him talking.

I asked Abraham what I could do for him. He continued looking at the floor and said nothing. Then I asked why he'd come for therapy but still no response was forthcoming. I asked him what he wanted to talk about – again nothing, just more silence. I feared that the silence would last till the end of the session. I was starting to panic and had no idea what to do next. Then the thought occurred to me that I shouldn't make any demands on him, that my questions were frightening him, and that most likely he was considerably more scared of me than I was of him. So together we sat in silence. Instinctively, I hadn't taken the chair next to the door, leaving that one for him. I was glad of this. He looked trapped and it seemed that flight had to be a realistic and available option if he were to feel safe enough to open up. I worried that he would just get up and leave and I really didn't want that to happen. I didn't want to fail this man, a man I'd only just met and knew nothing about.

After about fifteen minutes of sitting together, he raised his gaze for a brief moment, met my eyes fleetingly and looked down again. Then he looked up for a second, giving me a slightly longer glance. When he looked up a third time, I caught his eye and said: "Hello there." He said "Hi." That was it, until towards the end of the session when I again asked him how he was doing. He said he was OK. Then, after yet another, now more tolerable silence, he said that he'd come to counselling because he wanted to make his penis grow. He added that he also wanted to stop smoking. I asked him if he thought he might be able to talk to me about these things. He answered: "Yes, I think I can talk to you because you are a family man, and a Christian." The time was now up and as he stood to leave, he said: "I'll see you next week, same time." I was relieved and happy that we were going to meet again.

The following week I cycled up from Clapham. Waiting for him to arrive, I again felt unsure whether he'd turn up. The time to start had passed. When he finally entered the room, his anorak zipped and his hood up as before, I'd been waiting for over half an hour and had all but given up hope of seeing him. In the consulting room we took the same chairs. As another intense silence descended, I could feel my anxiety increasing. Then, in a voice so soft that I was forced to lean forward to hear, he began to speak.

A few weeks back he'd suffered a violent racial attack. London was changing into a more tolerant and cosmopolitan city in the 1980s; a multicultural revolution was taking place. The children of 1960s immigrants from the Indian sub-continent, Africa and the West Indies, born in Britain, now made up a noticeable proportion of the population. This reality delighted many, but some Londoners felt threatened by it and were angry. It was a dangerous time to be young, black and male. The police had recently intensified the government's notorious "stop and search" policy, which had the effect of targeting black men based on nothing more substantial than the colour of their skin. This in turn legitimised racial attacks by gangs of violent and often dispossessed white boys and men. The policy also made it extremely unlikely that any black male who'd been assaulted would seek protection or redress from the police.

Abraham had been set upon by a group of men, spat at, verbally abused, pushed to the ground, punched and kicked. He thought he was going to die. His ribs were badly bruised, he suffered many cuts and abrasions to his face and hands, his clothes were torn, and he was left half-conscious and covered in blood. Shockingly, no one came to his aid and since the attack he'd felt unsafe, suspicious and frightened of everyone. During the attack he'd felt paralysed, unable to put up any defence, and this left him feeling ashamed and weak, as if he were fair game for anyone wanting to beat, abuse or kill him. Even more disturbing, ever since his mind had been flooded with vivid thoughts and images of a man he'd known when he was a small child in Africa. These he experienced as dire warnings of imminent danger.

Abraham told me that he and his sister Sofia shared a flat in East London, but that since the assault he'd felt unsafe even inside this flat. He worried about break-ins and obsessively checked the locks on the doors and windows; from behind the curtains he scanned the street, expecting to see "him" watching, waiting. He could barely sleep and lost his appetite. He was also experiencing difficulty urinating. He was so fearful of imminent intrusion that he'd ceased washing, as removing any clothing would render him too vulnerable. He left the flat only when absolutely necessary, to go to work, to come to therapy, albeit in disguise, covered up. He was later to tell me that he envied how Muslim women could hide their bodies from the gaze of men behind the burka.

I began to get some understanding of the anorak and wondered how he was managing to summon up the courage to make it all the way across London to see me. Before he left the session, I asked him if it'd been me who'd mistaken the time of our meeting. In response he hesitated, then looked at me very directly and said that he knew the time of the appointment. No apology or explanation was forthcoming. When he left, I wrote "brave, self-contained, fiercely intelligent". It wasn't until much later that I realised just how apt that description was and just how much he was to teach me about trust.

Over the next few months, the sessions followed the same pattern. He always arrived late but unpredictably so, zipped up and hooded in the anorak. He uncovered his head only when we got into the room and I'd closed the door. For much of these early meetings neither of us spoke. Initially, I broke the silence, but when I mentioned this to Agnes, she told me to wait for him to speak, that my prompts might be having the effect of further shutting him down. I remember his reaction when I asked about the man who'd so frightened him. He stared at me wildly, the whites of his eyes growing even more prominent, so I backed off and he began to calm down. Direct questions had the effect of freezing him, threatening to damage any trust I'd earned. At times he seemed to find my presence baffling, surprising, even upsetting. During this time, Agnes's advice was again helpful and sustaining: "Just wait, step back, be patient, think your own thoughts, be curious about what comes up in your own mind, try not to speculate about him. Don't try to know and don't even think about trying to make any interpretations. You don't know what's going on in his mind, and it's a mistake to pretend to."

It wasn't until many weeks later, well into the autumn of that first year together, that he told me more about what had happened to him as a child. On that day he surprised me by arriving on time. It was clear that he was ready to begin, that he felt safe enough to start to talk about why he was so frightened.

Chapter Two

Healing Thyself

"I'll tell you what freedom is to me: no fear.
I mean really, no fear."

Nina Simone, interviewed in
New York, 1968

EVERY THERAPIST IS CHANGED BY THE people they
work with. But just occasionally, someone comes along
whose determination to find their way through suffering challenges us to rouse our own courage and go
beyond the limits of what we perceive to be comforta-
ble, known, or even possible. For me Abraham was just
such a person. We were to meet twice, and for a while,
three times a week, for over twelve years. He began to
tell me of the violence he'd been subjected to as a child.

He asked that I accompany him on a journey he knew he had to make into the darkness that had consumed and defined most of his life. One day he just came out with it.

A man, Abraham said, a trusted family watchman and guard, began to sexually abuse him when he was four years old. These assaults went on for the next four years and ceased only when the family moved to live in another country. But there again he was sexually abused, this time by an older cousin who raped him several times over the course of a year. When a violent revolution broke out in their homeland, the family was forced to flee and Abraham and Sofia found themselves separated from their parents and living as refugees in a children's home on the south coast of England. They were placed in local schools and it was there, at school, that he learned that if he was to keep safe, he must hide.

After briefly telling me of these events he shut down and reverted to coming to the sessions unpredictably late. No matter how gently and sensitively I enquired about the abuse, he refused to engage. He wasn't totally silent as when we first met, though, and told me bits about his life, including his job in the accounts department of a busy shipping firm. His desk was in an open-plan office but he tried to distance himself as much as possible from the general office banter and gossip that went on around him. He occasionally socialised with his sister's friends when she invited them to the flat they shared, but he had no friends of his own. The only other person he saw was his father, who lived in a council flat in another part of London. Abraham and his sister worried about him; they could see that he was drinking too much and becoming increasingly frail and depressed. Their father had not recovered from the shock of the revolution that had stripped him of everything and forced him into exile. All three were plagued by fear and uncertainty about the whereabouts of the children's mother. Nothing had been heard of her since she'd travelled back home after the coup d'état.

While the telling and retelling of such details of patients' lives are the meat and potatoes of therapy, there was something, both in the manner of Abraham's telling and in the content itself, that felt particularly hopeless and bleak. It was as if he knew he should talk about what was happening in his life but that somehow it was all irrelevant, that there was nothing either of us could say or do that would make any difference, would ever be able to ease the immense distress and loneliness in his life. He was very depressed, anxious and closed up, and while I was acutely aware of the weight of the suffering he'd endured and of the immense courage it had taken to come to therapy and speak of the abuse, I felt increasingly distracted and disconnected. I found it hard to focus and worried that I would fail him, that he would just cease coming and disappear without trace back into his life in East London. I was also frightened that, like so many hurting young men, he would take his own life – a life that seemed to be hanging together by the sheerest of threads.

On the few occasions when he referred to the abuse in the ensuing sessions, it was as if he was telling me about things that happened to someone else, not him, not the man sitting right in front of me. I couldn't understand what was happening. It had taken months to win his confidence and I could feel that connection slipping away. I felt impatient and at times I sensed his irritation, and my own. When I lost the thread of what he was saying and sought clarification he became frustrated – with both my failure to hold the narrative and his own inarticulacy. He was tighter and more closed than ever.

* * *

We were both trying hard. Too hard. I, to understand and help him, and he to navigate his way in therapy, through a new and one-sided relationship with a stranger. He later told me that my good intentions, my feeling sorry for him, got in the way. It was only after we had been apart for three weeks in late autumn 1989, after the death of my father, that things began to shift.

My father had been ill with heart problems for years and had recently suffered a devastating stroke that had rendered him unable to move or speak. It was clear that he was dying. I flew to Toronto and found myself alone in the hospital room with him. There, too, I felt locked in and inadequate. I found I was unable to feel, communicate or comfort him in any way, even to hold his hand or tell him how much I loved him. In the face of his dying, I froze. I felt cold, distant and frightened. I sat beside his death bed waiting for any opportunity to escape.

As father and son, we'd not always had an easy time of it. I had adored him when I was a child. He was a gentle, affectionate and imaginative father but as I entered adulthood, he found me perplexing, my opinions and lifestyle confusing and disappointing. What he gleaned of my sexuality disturbed him. I forced myself to turn away from him while still aware and pained by my need and love for him. Partly in reaction to this seeming rejection, I left Canada and moved to the UK, a place where I knew no one and, importantly, no one knew me, and where I could come out as gay.

And now suddenly he was gone – and I was in turmoil. For many years I had resented him and fought against him, reacting to what I experienced as his disapproval. Artificially bolstered by my rather sensitive ego, I had thought him weak, envious and pathetic. But his dying had been so brutal and terrifying that all I could think of was how lonely he must have been, how he'd needed my love and kindness in those last years, and then last hours, of his life, and that I had failed him. Shortly after arriving back in London, I fell into a savage depression.

I had been depressed before but had always managed to get out of it, to avoid facing what I needed to face, by changing scene, by moving, travelling to different countries. But now the option of escape did not seem to present itself.

As part of my therapy training, I was in therapy myself but had so far managed to evade being subjected to any deep scrutiny. I had from early on, like Abraham, learned how to hide and I didn't know how to stop. It prevented me from addressing my suffering or making use of the help I was being offered. I seriously considered ending my training. The very idea that I could help someone as hurt as Abraham struck me forcefully as ridiculous and arrogant, not to mention fraudulent.

* * *

It was around this time that my partner suggested that we go and listen to a talk by a Tibetan Buddhist teacher. I was reluctant. Growing up Catholic, I'd had enough of religion and was resistant to the idea that spirituality had anything to offer me, but he was insistent, and I grudgingly curious. After a long wait, an Asian man dressed in a light-blue suit arrived on stage. He sat down on a brocade-covered chair, took a long drink from a glass of a clear liquid that might have been water or even straight vodka, and for some minutes, said nothing. He just looked at us with a broad smile on his face. He pondered the glass on the side table, slowly picked it up, and took another sip. He then placed it carefully back down. He again looked at us, and again smiled. All this seemed to take an eternity but was somehow fascinating and engaging. I was mesmerised by the stillness and the spaciousness that seemed to surround him and by the elegance of his movements, so much so that, when he finally did speak, I jumped. I'll never forget his words, although I didn't understand them at the time. Even now, many years later, they still have a meaning that I find I'm only occasionally able to grasp. He simply said: "Ladies and Gentlemen, I must tell you, there are no reference points." He then repeated this sentence one more time, took another long, elegant sip from the glass, placed it carefully back on the side table next to a strikingly simple flower arrangement, and in a high-pitched voice asked if there were any questions. That was it, that was the talk.

I can't remember the few questions that were asked, nor do I recall his very brief answers. But I do recall feeling increasingly uncomfortable and curiously angry. I'd never experienced anything so odd or so powerful. I can only describe my reaction as feeling somehow "bitten". I signed up for the course he was teaching the following weekend, in which he gave three talks. He was warm, kind and gently animated, and while he was in the room, there was no possibility of hiding. His message was very simple and unlike any religious teaching I'd ever heard. There was nothing fearful or judgemental, no place to get to, nothing to achieve, nothing to improve. I was being told to trust myself, to relax, to enjoy being myself. What I heard him saying was that I must experience "NO struggle". As he spoke these words, I simultaneously felt both the heaviness of all the complication and distress I had mistakenly identified as intrinsically me and a distinct separation from all that struggle. I had the thought: this is what freedom must feel like, being totally, nakedly and completely relaxed, stripped of the usual defences yet free of fear, of shame, feeling only warmth and release.

As I write this, it occurs to me that the effect of being close to this man was possibly my first conscious experience of what Abraham and I would come to call "undressing". That is, of being stripped of negative judgments, self-criticism, shame and fear of oneself and others, and most importantly, experiencing just being. It wasn't so much that I had been seen and accepted by someone else – this Buddhist teacher – rather that I could glimpse myself as good, as intrinsically just fine. It was a foretaste, a strong, slightly out-of-focus image, a perception, a change in perspective. I had definitely glimpsed it, and that glimpse would change everything.

* * *

Abraham was also undergoing change. He started to speak about the effects of what the abusers had done to him. He felt he was inhabited by something rotten and unpalatable. He described how he experienced "the world from the outside-in" as opposed to "inside-out". He was certain that people saw him as repulsive, as something dirty, someone to be shunned. He suspected this to be a skewed image, that was based on the words and actions of the men who abused him, but it was nevertheless insistent and overwhelming. He spoke of needing to challenge this perception, but he didn't know how or if it was even possible.

Chapter Three

A Garden in Africa

"You've got to be taught to hate and fear."

Rodgers and Hammerstein,
South Pacific, 1949

THE STORIES COME OUT IN FRAGMENTS. Like photos fallen from an old family album and then blown about by a chance wind. And yet the growing trust between us creates a slight feeling of leisureliness, almost a sense of calm, as we allow the jumble of scenes and experiences to begin to take their own shape and tell us what they will, in their own time.

His parents are wealthy and larger than life, yet also remote, unknowable. He cannot remember any particular instances of being cuddled or even touched by either father or mother. They are around only infrequently and mostly live and work abroad in the diplomatic service. From a very early age he has been left in the care of his father's mother and an unmarried aunt. His grandmother is frail and bed-ridden but he knows she loves him, and he in turn loves her.

His family lives in the wealthy area of a large African city. High walls topped with broken glass and razor wire surround a compound and a garden; a sentry box is manned day and night by armed guards, paid protection against the envy and struggle enveloping the rest of the city. From down the road come the smells and the noise of that mêlée: the traffic and shouting, the heavy mist of diesel fumes, the cooking oils and smoke that belch out from hearths in thousands of tin shack homes. Food is constantly being boiled, baked and fried. There are markets where stacks of oily fish tumble from trays, hunks of fly-blackened meats hang on steel hooks, stalls heave with vegetables, sacks of rice and mountains of colourful spices, all waiting to be haggled over. Brightly dressed women balance their purchases on their heads, leaving their hands free to tightly hold their precious offspring. There are edges and precipices everywhere: graveyards are overflowing with the bodies of children who were unable to keep up, who slipped the grasp of desperate parents. In the air there are also stirrings of further conflict. Men are arming themselves, covertly planning, promising freedom, land reform, lower prices, fairness, cheap food, an end to the rich, democracy. It is a call to arms that will deliver the usual cruelty, the unthinking violence and yet another version of unfairness into the fragile lives of those struggling to survive.

But within the wealthy compound all is seemingly safe and calm. There are water sprinklers keeping the lawns green and the gardens flowering; there is an order that disguises the dangers to be found even here. A woman, his aunt, driven half-mad by forces not dissimilar to those about to prey upon her charge, sits upright under an umbrella, a holy book in her lap. The child tries with little success to attract her attention, to engage her in some game or other. To her, his questions are a distraction. He is curious about everything, the names of trees, of flowers, of insects, and he wants her to read to him. She mistrusts this curiosity and is infuriated by the questions: "Why this? Why that? How come this? How come that?" She protects herself from her loneliness with a set of fierce evangelical certainties and is continually on the lookout for sinful impulses. His questions are evidence of just such devilish foolishness.

She is also resentful at having this "spoiled" child as her only company. Ignored and pushed away, he becomes fractious, demanding and sulky; he is a bad boy distracting her from her prayers, her mission, her ultimate salvation. Eventually, at her wits' end, she locks him in a dark, windowless garden hut, warning him against crying, complaining or throwing a tantrum. She tells him that if he makes any noise the devil will come and get him.

But he does cry out, and he is frightened of the darkness. He begs to be let out of this hot smelly prison. His aunt goes indoors to be away from this bawling. And shortly, as his aunt has predicted, someone does appear in the doorway. But it's not the devil. He knows this man. He's one of the watchmen, a familiar face, one of the men who keep the family safe, who guard the grounds from dangerous intruders. Briefly his hopes are raised. This particular man has been kind, he has patiently answered his questions. His visit seems a welcome surprise. The watchman has heard his cries and come to help him, to protect him, to release him from the darkness.

Abraham's relief quickly turns to confusion when the man begins to act strangely. Rather than let him out of the hut, he shuts the door behind him, and, without uttering a word, he starts to caress him; he strokes his head, his arms and his legs. He seems to be touching him everywhere. Abraham has stopped crying but doesn't like being touched. The man undoes his own trousers and tells him to touch his penis. Abraham does as he's told and the man seems pleased. But then he takes hold of Abraham's head and puts his penis into Abraham's mouth. Abraham finds this very uncomfortable. It makes him feel sick. He is also very confused. Somehow, he knows that what the watchman is doing isn't just strange, it's wrong. He starts to panic. He fears he'll choke to death and wants this new game to stop. He struggles to get free, but the man's grip tightens. Finally, after what seems like ages, the man lets go of him. But now the man is angry. He again grabs the boy's face and orders him to keep quiet, not to tell anyone. He threatens to kill him along with his aunt and grandmother if he utters one word. Then he whispers: "If you tell, it will never grow!"

The watchman leaves Abraham locked in the shed again. The panic and confusion he felt as the watchman forced his mouth open are now accompanied by a new feeling, one that he doesn't at first recognise or understand, but one with which he will become very familiar. His aunt's warning seems to have come true. This is what happens to bad boys. He knows he's crossed some line and that there is no going back, to safety or to home. He feels something is overwhelming him. His mind is wild with it, his body jittery with it. He fears he'll die of it. But he also knows that he must get these feelings under control. When his aunt comes to release him, he must act as if nothing has happened. He must show no sign.

As Abraham tells me about what was done to him as a small child, I hold his gaze. The air in the room is thick with tension. What he is describing doesn't seem so much an account of past events but something witnessed, experienced in the room in front of us, now. I feel frightened and overwhelmed but also protective, a parent trying to comfort an inconsolable child. It is as if the abuser has gotten into our room; we can feel his presence, smell him everywhere. There is no escape; something has been let out and can't be put back in.

Abraham asks if I am OK; should he go on? And from then on, at the end of each session, he asks if it's alright if he comes back next week. His wariness and silence over the previous months have not solely been about self-protection. He also wants to keep me safe, unpolluted. He is uncertain as to whether I am able to tolerate what he has to tell me, whether I care enough to hear him out, to stay with him. He has been fighting a great prohibition on telling and feels ashamed of what he has to say of himself. Much later, he would speak of the terror at breaking the silence. "I think I'm only now beginning to realise that I've been afraid my whole life; I can't imagine what it's like not to be afraid. For so long I've thought I should kill myself, that I want to be dead, to kill off these feelings." At this point I told him that I wanted to see him more often, that once a week made it too long a stretch between sessions. His relief at hearing this was palpable.

Chapter Four

Permission to Speak

*"Freedom's possibility is not the ability to choose the good
or the evil... it is the possibility to be able."*

The Concept of Anxiety,
Søren Kierkegaard, 1844

"IF YOU TELL, IT WILL NEVER GROW!" This threat, first
heard when he was four years old and drummed into
him by the watchman over many years, lodged itself
in Abraham's psyche as something both enigmatic and
unquestionably certain. This seven-word threat uncan-
nily sums up the nature of the entrapping dilemma
faced by abused children and the adults they grow into.
Such a threat absolves the abuser of responsibility and
passes it on to the child. In consequence, the child's

capacity to think, remember and speak is broken by the weight of guilt and shame. The adult has seized the high ground by appropriating the role of rule maker.

* * *

One of the first times we met, before he'd even told me of the abuse, Abraham said that what concerned him most about coming to therapy was that it might involve "telling". He both feared and longed for the release that telling might produce yet couldn't begin to imagine how sentences could be formed, how to make any sense of the chaos of his thoughts, feelings and memories. In the end what made telling possible for him was rendering the listener, me, safe. He made me a man with uncomplicated desires and consigned these to marriage and to the rearing of children circumscribed by the laws of God. In that first session when I enquired whether he thought he could talk to me about quitting smoking and making his penis grow, he had answered: "Yes, because you are a Christian and a family man."

As well as rendering me benign, Abraham was unconsciously backing a fundamentalist viewpoint in a polarised debate about the development of sexual desire. Put simply, the debate is about whether human sexual desire comes from the inside or the outside. Is it a product of nature or nurture, a biologically defined urge inherent at birth or something that is worked on, developed, directed and at times misdirected by encounters with others? For Abraham there was nothing theoretical or esoteric about this debate; rather it was a source of great worry and confusion. If his sexuality were inherent, then he feared he must be homosexual. This disturbed him because in his eyes it suggested that he had an inherent desire to engage in sex with men, and more worryingly, with the men who abused him. On the other hand, if sexual desire could be formed by another, by "nurture" then the words of the abuser, "If you tell, it will never grow", took on added significance. They would have the power to form him, keep him forever small, immature and thus excluded from adult relationships.

The threat "If you tell, it will never grow!" also contained its own internal explosive charge, set to go off by the mere thought of telling. Abraham spoke of being sure that he somehow gave off an odour that only men who wished to abuse him could smell. He believed that these men could identify the "victim" in him, and he feared that they would be able to sniff out his vulnerability, his availability and his tainted desire for them.

He knew that he was unable to defend himself against their advances and further abuse, trapped as he was in collusive silence. The abuser's words locked him into an impossible dilemma, putting speech at odds with sexual development. The terrible complication of this perverted logic kept him forever the vulnerable child, frozen in time, an un-kissed, imprisoned Sleeping Beauty.

Conversely, not telling left him weighed down with responsibility for the abuse. The fact that he had done nothing to stop either the watchman or his older cousin from abusing him again and again made him anxious. The inference he drew from this was that he'd brought it upon himself. He must have wanted it and was perversely excited by and drawn to men who could overpower him. He was troubled that it had happened with two different men, that he had gone from being abused by one man to being raped by another, to being bullied at school by bigger boys, and more recently to passively undergoing the racial attack in London that had finally brought him to my office.

After the first abuser had forbidden him from speaking out, it had rendered any chance of protesting, of protecting himself, of saying "No!", impossible. In a paper entitled "The Capacity to be Alone", the British psychoanalyst and paediatrician Donald Winnicott, who died in 1971 but whose writings continue to inspire, guide and sustain the work of many therapists and analysts today, asserted that the capacity for both verbal and sexual development is facilitated by an environment of trust. Children who are trusted to think for themselves by a confident parent develop the capacity to be alone, to be free, to think their own thoughts, to be creative, to be themselves. A lovely example of this capacity is often cited: a child is standing alone in a room looking out at the night sky, totally immersed in his or her own thoughts. A parent enters. The trusted child will continue to be spellbound, aware but not disrupted by the intrusion, while the mistrusted child's attention will be kidnapped by concern and anxiety. The quote by Kierkegaard at the beginning of this chapter points to the same truth: freedom is the capacity to be able. Able to choose, able to feel, able to explore, able to play, but also able to think and to speak for oneself without feeling the undue influence of others.

Perhaps the development of sexual choice and desire mirrors the development of speech. Speech comes as a surprise in the very young, as does crawling and then walking. But there quickly comes a time when the will of the child takes over as they try to make sense of their experience of the world. They begin to express likes and dislikes, to protest and demand, to respond verbally to and with others. We know that a responsive parent can speed up and direct this process, as a non-responsive, impatient or depressed parent can impede it. Perhaps the same is simultaneously true with the development of sexual desire and preference. The discovery of sexual desire and choice also seems to come as a surprise. It's as if we wake up to something we've always known but haven't had the capacity to articulate.

The thinking behind the Thatcher government's implementation of Clause 28 in 1988, which outlawed any discussion and teaching about homosexuality in schools, was based upon the idea that sexual preference was a matter of influence. It was believed that simply speaking about same-sex desire was somehow promoting it. Silencing free speech was the modus operandi of this foolish piece of legislation. We see this same logic wreaking still more vicious havoc and oppression today in Putin's Russia. Both cases are examples of abuse and violations of human rights.

Abuse overpowers and disrupts the capacity to think and to speak for oneself. It stupefies the individual's capacity to communicate, verbally, emotionally and creatively – that is its aim. Abraham was silenced, and this locked him into an intimate relationship with his abusers; he was left sharing secrets only with them. Given this dilemma, he avoided and feared familiarity with anyone outside this dreadful collusion. In the consulting room, he was suspicious of our growing intimacy. He was forever on the lookout for signs of my disgust, my disapproval. And he suspected my silences, moments when I was thoughtful or uncertain, as evidence of my being overwhelmed by him and the terrible "stinking mess" inside him. He also feared that I would think him pitiful, weak, a victim, but above all, complicit in the abuse – and consider him either mad or bad. He feared that he would fail. Fail me, fail himself, fail in therapy, fail in life and in love.

Chapter Five

On Fear and Responsibility

"I assess the power of a will by how much resistance,
pain, torture it endures and knows how to turn
to its advantage."
Friedrich Nietzsche, *The Will to Power*, 1901

VERY FEW, IF ANY OF US, depart childhood unscathed
or unafraid. Indeed, it seems that fear is ubiquitous,
a major component of sentience. Fear is cyclical; it
begets more fear, one fear leading on to another. In *An
Outline of Psychoanalysis* (1938), Freud wrote that very
young children enter into an unconscious bargain with
their parents; a bargain designed to keep them safe. In
this scenario, protection is maintained by means of the
child's compliance, their maintaining "good-enough

behaviour" and the capacity of the parent to tolerate the child's demands. This arrangement can be experienced as a threat and weigh heavily on some children. They fear that failure to comply may result in withdrawal of love and security and make them vulnerable "to the dangers of the external world…" Life becomes precarious and anxiety grows.

But what happens to the child when those "dangers of the external world" do break through as they did with Abraham? When I first met him, Abraham often spoke of living in a kind of prison, a place where he was both prison guard and inmate. He inhabited a world populated by victims and abusers and was threatened by an environment of impending horror. He was on constant alert and felt responsible for everything and everyone. With every lapse in this vigilant watchfulness he became harshly self-critical.

But as our meetings continued, he became aware of small gaps in his usual state of hyper-vigilance. These were moments when his attention was distracted, and he found himself almost trusting, almost relaxing in the session. But when he noticed what was happening, he quickly pulled back from the brink and immediately sealed himself back up in a flurry of self-criticism. One bodily manifestation of this hyper-vigilance and control was paruresis, sometimes called shy bladder syndrome, the inability to urinate in public places. For Abraham, this was triggered by the thought of being seen touching his penis, caught in the act of masturbation, the victim of male attention. In this drama there was no place for relaxation or trust. He had to stay clenched as if his life depended on it. Instead of letting himself go and urinating, he became flooded with angry and paranoid thoughts and the sphincter controlling urination tightened. No matter how full his bladder or how urgent the demand, he was unable to let go. The more urgent the need to pee, the more constricted the sphincter. This condition caused him serious distress as well as terrible pain. It consumed his entire day, and as it entailed the very flow of life, the intake and outflow of liquids, it had severe consequences for his health.

* * *

To understand the roots of this blockage, we must engage with the second round of abuse that befell him. At the age of eight, Abraham was still subject to the watchman's demands and despaired that anything would change. His parents – blithely unaware of their son's problem – took him to live with them abroad. There he joined his elder sister Sofia, other members of his extended family, in an embassy house in Europe. This reunion gave him respite from what had been taking place in the garden hut, and allowed him a brief, unfamiliar taste of companionship and safety. It was at first a relief, especially to have the company of his sister, with whom he was developing what would become a vital and lasting bond. He relished the opportunity to attend a real school and play with other children. He spoke of how much he enjoyed the games he and Sofia played, almost forgetting the darkness and the secret prohibition "on telling" to which he was subject. But this brief interlude was not to last.

The grooming started when he expressed an interest in the act of kissing. Abraham had seen his cousin, a man of eighteen, kissing a girl and wondered what it might feel like. The young man befriended him but then used his expression of curiosity as a pretext to control him. First, he instructed Abraham in the practice of kissing. Secret venues were found for this practice, and again Abraham was told he must tell no one, that if it were to get out both would get into trouble, that Abraham would certainly be sent back to Africa in disgrace. These meetings led to Abraham being inducted into more invasive sexual acts, masturbating his cousin and giving him oral sex, then finally to being violently raped. The first rape happened at an embassy party. It took place in a bathroom, against a sink. Abraham recounted that he could hear his mother's laughter through the wall while the assault was taking place. The juxtaposition of being so painfully violated by a member of his family, within hearing of his mother's joviality, intensified his distress. The paruresis was a consequence of this rape.

And once again, Abraham found himself ensnared by another man's words. This time the threat used was different, and in some ways, more insidious: "If you tell you'll never kiss a girl." These words trapped him in another impossible dilemma, an impasse that would further confuse and block his development. "Am I gay or straight? If I tell anyone, if word gets out that I've been raped, they'd think I wanted it, that I must have made him do it. He was handsome and my mother really seems to like him. I'd be the one called a homosexual, and in my country, they kill homosexuals."

His mother, a wealthy landowner and diplomat in her own right, was by Abraham's admission not very motherly. He felt that, while being known as a mother gave her kudos, her children somehow cramped her style. The occasion of the rape confirmed that he could not count on her. This hard lesson meant that keeping silent was a choice-less reality. He was forced to learn to hide, to suffer alone and in secret. He said that it was then that everything had changed. He realised that there was no safety to be had anywhere. He could find no escape and no refuge. He began consciously to over-dress, to cover up, to avoid others, avoid public places and any activity that required undressing – so no swim-ming and no sleepovers.

When he told me of the rape all those years later, he said that he often got terrible shooting pains in his legs and backside and that he could still feel the man's penis lodged inside him. It felt like something was stuck there, something foreign, disgusting. He said he wasn't capable of dislodging it and told me of the physical pain it caused him, which made it difficult to think. There was too much distress, too much feeling. But then during one session, something took place that unexpectedly gave him some relief. In the session I sim-ply asked him to tell me of the overwhelming feeling that he was experiencing at that moment. He imme-diately said: "Fear". I asked him to tell me whose fear it was that he was feeling. "My own, of course." This exchange led on to us speaking about responsibility. We talked about the fact that even though what happened to him was not his responsibility, or his fault, he did bear responsibility for how he dealt with it and for his own feelings. This recognition had a profound effect upon us both. It broke the spell and suddenly we had something to talk about and indeed to do.

At the start of the next session, Abraham said he'd given more thought to our discussion about responsibility. He said that for so long he'd been ensnared by the words of his abusers. These threats had confused and trapped him into taking all the burden of responsibility for what these men did to him. I said something like: "Maybe that was what the men wanted you to do?" He thought that was right. I then said that perhaps this transferral of blame was a crime in some ways more terrible than the actual physical abuse. "You have been trapped in confusion for so many years, unable to see how insane it is that you have taken all the responsibility for what happened – but it isn't your insanity, it's theirs." He simply said: "It's time for me to change things around! I suddenly feel even more scared and I wonder why… But I also feel less confused and I can see that I'm afraid of my own fear." That realisation was to make everything different and everything possible.

Chapter Six

Ritual and Resistance

*"Ritual: an outer framework which both occasions
and identifies an inner event."*
Iris Murdoch, *The Sovereignty of Good*, 1970

THE SEEDS OF OUR LONGING FOR freedom are often
to be found in the way we resist. For the first five
years, Abraham was never or very rarely on time for
our sessions. The timing of his arrival was impossible
to predict. Sometimes he arrived five minutes late and
at other times with only five minutes to go. I initially
thought that this lateness was a problem reflecting
on my therapeutic skill. I felt the need to keep both
of us within the discipline of the therapeutic model.
He quietly resisted this demand, leaving me at times

feeling bewildered and impotent. But this seemingly cavalier attitude to time helped him to preserve something essential. Slowly, I was forced to give up hope that he would ever comply to the "rules" of the game of therapy, and my frustration was replaced by a grudging respect for his stubborn determination not to submit. Had I succeeded in forcing his compliance, I now firmly believe that he would have felt manipulated and stifled. He was starting to do things his own way, creating the therapy he needed and not complying with the one that was on offer. I realised that my role in his therapy, although crucial, was simply to offer a place for us to think together, but then to get out of his way when it was time for action.

* * *

Early on in my life, I too had schooled myself in non-compliance. By the age of nine, this refusal had resulted in my having failed three years of primary school. In those days, each failure meant being held back an entire year, so that at nine years old, I was sitting in class with children of seven. I was left effectively illiterate, unable to read or write until I approached puberty.

My fear and silence were routinely mistaken for

stupidity or insolence. I was always the oldest, biggest, dumbest kid in the class. One year, my only competitor for that honour, and my ally, was an immigrant boy whose family had just arrived from Italy, who was able to speak only basic English. We were seated together at the back of the class so as to not get in the way of the brighter, more articulate children. What I needed was gentleness, kindly interest and a great deal of one-to-one attention and encouragement. But those were vastly different times, so instead I was punished. Beatings, face slaps, put-downs, ritual public humiliations and an array of imaginatively bizarre tortures were commonplace in Catholic schools at that time. One particularly sadistic punishment – one more recently used in Guantanamo Bay – had the child kneeling on the floor, hands behind his back, leaning into a wall, his forehead and neck forced to suffer the weight of his body.

I developed severe migraines. The nuns were the worst culprits, and they were in charge. Even then I was aware that the non-religious teachers were also intimidated by the nuns' severity, as were my parents. No one protested. As in Ireland, where many of them came from, the priests and nuns exercised the right to enter the family home to ensure Catholic teachings were being followed. In my case, they reported back about "wilful disobedience" at school to my parents, who were made to feel ashamed of my "behaviour". The Church exerted great influence.

There was no escape and so I, like so many others, lived on my nerves, hiding, trying to keep my head down, endeavouring to reduce myself to nothing. If I was called upon to answer a question or read something aloud in class, I sometimes pissed myself. I remember feeling hot, claustrophobic, visceral, clammy and sinful. The strap – a leather and wire contraption used to beat the hands of small children, sometimes till they bled – and the stick, were common educational tools. Like most masochists, I saw a good beating as my just deserts, absolving me of my sin of failure, "outing" me for my sticky weirdness. It relieved the pressure of having to hide. My failure upset my parents. I experienced it as a moral failing and every week I tried to attain the status of a good Catholic boy by confessing my sins to the priest. I was given a penance in atonement and told I needed to try harder to be good. I thought of the lives of the Christian martyrs, their suffering described in pornographically exciting detail in one of the few books we had at home, egging me on to see just how much abuse I could take. It was my version of cutting or self-harm –

having a similar effect of relieving pressure and letting out some of my "badness". Yet as with other forms of self-abuse, it became compulsive and locked me into the perverse logic of good and bad, right and wrong meted out by the Church.

I passionately hated school and learning and, in consequence, my own mind. Probably these were my only passions, apart from worrying about my daily stomach aches and keeping a hawk's eye on my mother's moods, to try and work out whether I was in or out of favour. She was at that time struggling with her own anxiety. She was raised the only child of older parents, both of whom had died by her middle twenties, her father in an insane asylum after a breakdown caused by a financial collapse, and her mother after developing a form of early-onset senility. She then married and, with breakneck speed, got pregnant eight times, producing seven children in just over ten years. She was a remarkably dutiful and responsible mother, and – crucially for the sanity of all of her children – a very present and loving one.

But we were a priest-ridden family. My parents didn't entirely trust their own natural sanity and goodness and were ensnared in trying to be good Catholic parents. As in most families, it is the unacknowledged secrets and lies that have the power to sway, divert and undermine confidence and trust. Our family's big secret was that our father's mother, a warm and eccentric woman who lived with us, was in fact not Catholic by birth, as everyone was led to believe, but Jewish. This was a self-secret, one we kept from ourselves, something we children half-consciously knew but never articulated. To be Catholic or Protestant, English, Scottish or Irish in the Toronto of that era was normal; to be Jewish, black or gay was simply impossible. Prejudice was rife and considered honourable and sensible. I never wondered about the *gefilte-fish* (stuffed fish), the matza-balls, the *krautstruedel* (cabbage pie) and the delicious chicken soup with dumplings served up by my grandmother, nor the Yiddish exclamations, the "*Oy gevalts*" and the "*Oy veihs*". I was far too busy being a disappointment to notice that in this rather significant matter we were different from the other Irish Catholic families.

Meanwhile, I continued to fail or attain the barest of possible passes at tests in school, and it was taking a heavy toll on me both physically and emotionally. Then, quite unexpectedly, when I was sixteen, I cracked. But instead of having the expected breakdown, I suddenly found my voice, and that voice was surprisingly angry and self-empowering. I had been suffering through yet another class overseen by yet another conflicted priest who was making his way along the aisles of teenage boys looking for miscreants to punish. He spotted the mess I was making of a Latin translation. He raised the stick, his eyes seeming to sparkle with pleasurable anticipation of the hurt and shame he was about to inflict. This particular time, however, something primitive and uncomplicated erupted within me: disgust – only this time not for myself, but for him. In that instant I'd had enough. Grabbing the cane from his hands, I hurled it out of an open window and walked away from that school and, as I hoped, the Catholic Church for ever.

If only it were that easy! I would like to report that this act of rebellion got me out of the reach of priests, but this has proved to be a lifelong struggle. Priests come in many guises and old habits die hard. Nevertheless, for the first time, I felt free to trust myself. It gave me a taste of freedom, freedom to poke my head out from under all that shame and religious mumbo-jumbo. It felt very good. And surprisingly right. The following week, I enrolled in the high school down the road, the one we Catholics had been taught to call the "Protestant" school, although it was in fact just an ordinary Toronto secondary school. My parents didn't question my decision, nor did they reprimand me or force me to return to the hated Catholic school as instructed by the priests. For this, and much more, I am eternally grateful.

At the new school, I was taught by two wonderful women for two gloriously reparative years: Mrs Leach, who taught English Literature, and Mrs Botterell, who taught History. Almost fifty years later, I can still weep with relief and gratitude for their kindness, sensitivity and brilliance. They gave me my first real experience of intellectual and aesthetic pleasure and an appreciation for my own mind. They calmed me. I soon realised that I wasn't stupid, but simply rigid with fear. I remember Mrs Leach telling me early on that I would need to work very hard to catch up, because, as she succinctly put it: "Those Catholics, they haven't taught you anything." In her class we studied seduction poetry. She met hormonally fired teenagers halfway, educating us to investigate our own desires, and to learn about the desires of others, appreciate that others had desires. She introduced us to the work of John Donne, "the young rake", whose poems were about the biting of fleas, the mingling of bodily fluids, about love and desire and death; to Marvell's "Coy Mistress", Lawrence's "Snake", and Auden's call to his boy lover to "lay your sleeping head" upon his faithless arm, and to Shakespeare's erotically charged, heart-rending sonnets expressing the pain and the joy of love for both women and men. We learned of mutability, the awareness of death as a call to living fully rather than as a source of threat to be good and keep your head down. All this filled me with excitement. Here were sex and aliveness, desire and urgency, accompanied by the command to live life fully, to love and learn; stories of men wanting women, women desiring men, men for men, women for women, bodies bringing joy to other bodies, enjoying having a body! It was written down: it wasn't hidden, sin or pornography – as my former Catholic teachers would have it – but art. It was taught with playfulness, humour and seriousness and I had permission to enjoy, indeed, to learn from it. When we were given licence to write our own seduction poems, she played recordings of Andrés Segovia and Jascha Heifetz. Then Mrs Botterell brought the history of the twentieth century to life, cutting through our provincialism with stories of people pitted against tyrants. We read of the fight against Nazism and the horrors of the Holocaust, the crushing of the brave in the Warsaw uprising, of Stalin's purges and of the gulags, and of the show trials of Joe McCarthy right on our doorstep. I was being taught about repression and had my own personal experience of what that felt like, but also, now, of what freedom might feel like. A bigger world was opening up and I was being allowed and encouraged to partake.

* * *

One day, Abraham quite unexpectedly arrived on time and announced that he needed to get circumcised. Contrary to local custom, his father had neglected to have him circumcised in infancy. This failure seemed to fit with what he'd told me of his parents. They were both on their second marriages, and had several children each, by different partners, Abraham and Sofia being the only children of this marriage. When he was six or seven, his father realised his oversight in not having arranged the circumcision and began to make plans. But by that time, unbeknownst to anyone, Abraham was already being abused by the watchman, and when he was told of the operation, he had started to scream and begged his father to leave him alone. His grandmother told his father that it was too late for him to be trying to correct his mistakes and oversights. His father backed down, accusing his son of cowardice, threatening that he would be a laughing stock, never a proper man and forever undesirable to women, unwittingly echoing the threats of the abuser: "If you tell, it will never grow!"

In our sessions at that time, Abraham asked me if I thought he should go ahead with the surgery. The operation was expensive and painful for a grown man; but was it necessary? What would I do in his place? It was the first time he had asked for my advice. I responded by saying that maybe this question was more about making his own decision but I'd try to help him decide. He asked if it was about being brave, about being a real man. I told him I thought that these two things weren't always the same, that bravery was something that you could develop, while being a man was just an accident of birth. He seemed genuinely confused by what seemed blindingly obvious, so I asked him if he had any thoughts about courage. He said he wouldn't know, because he was a coward. I told him that I couldn't disagree more, that I experienced him as one of the bravest men I knew and that his coming to therapy was a huge act of courage. "But," he answered, "how can I be brave when I'm so frightened all the time?" I said that everyone was frightened. The only difference was that some people were brave enough to admit it and I knew he was a very brave man. This pleased and confused him in equal measure. For so long, he had been convinced that others could only see him as he experienced himself and to think otherwise was disorienting.

As we spoke of his father's failure to have him circumcised in infancy, the implications of this oversight grew. Circumcision, in his as in many cultures, is a ritual confirming the infant boy's entry into membership of the tribe, a ceremonial embracing and taking of him under its protection. It is also a proclamation of paternity. "This boy is my son and he is a member of our tribe, and this ritual marks this and honours him as such." Abraham had noticed he was different from other boys and saw this as another reflection of his own weakness and isolation, of his failure to be accepted and seen as being worthy of entering into the world of men, celebrated by the men of his own culture. As we explored what this meant, it dawned upon him that it was not his fault but was in fact a profound failure on the part of his father. He began to feel angry and dishonoured. And yet he couldn't quite let go of the idea that his father's neglect was symbolic of his low status. He wondered if the men who had abused him could somehow "recognise" this, had read it as an invitation to use his unclaimed, unfathered and unprotected body as they wished. As these thoughts began to sink in, he became certain that circumcision was an absolute necessity, an essential move towards the claiming back of his own body, his own genitals, and furthermore of his own mind.

Over the next few weeks, the themes of ritual and circumcision were the main foci of our sessions. He wanted to mark his body, as with a tattoo, to mark it as his, to remind himself that despite all that had been taken from him and irrespective of his thoughts and memories, it was his body. The novelist and philosopher Iris Murdoch wrote in *The Sovereignty of Good*, a collection of her essays published in 1970, of the need for ritual in our lives: they act as public displays that can point to – and thus also enable – inner changes. Abraham's healing came about partly due to his ability to invent a succession of highly personal rituals for himself, each of which was to make possible a fresh perspective.

He hesitated for three or four weeks. He then booked the appointment. On that day, just hours after the surgery, he arrived for his session in great pain but beaming with pride. I had never seen him look so pleased with himself and I was immensely proud of him too. I also recognised, from my own experience, how exhilarating it feels to suddenly find that one has the power to act in one's own best interest. He'd done it, by and for himself and for the first time in his life he got a taste of what freedom felt like.

Chapter Seven

A Room of One's Own

"Our most profound experiences are physical events."
Richard Ford, *Canada*, 2012

ABRAHAM'S CIRCUMCISION WAS A SIGNIFICANT TURNING point which led swiftly to the next development. A few weeks later, he announced that he'd applied for and, after many months of waiting, been offered an unfurnished bedsit by a local housing association. Since leaving school he had been sharing the same one-bedroom flat in East London with his sister Sofia. They had been brought to the UK by their father, when Abraham was nine and Sofia ten, following the coup that made returning home unsafe. Soon after their arrival in London, their father had declared himself incapable of providing a home for his children and social services had installed them in a hostel for refugee children on the south coast of England. Sofia was very much the "older sister" to Abraham, comforting and standing up for him, and offering him as much protection as she was able in this new and at times hostile environment. It was after she had left school and moved to London that he was to suffer the most intense and vicious bullying at school. As soon as he was legally able to leave school, he too headed for London and moved into Sofia's flat, where he once again found refuge under the watchful care of his beloved older sister.

But now some ten years later, he needed his own place. He knew that in order for things to change he had to begin the practice of undressing. Since leaving school, Abraham had never been fully naked – not even in the shower. This self-imposed prohibition made his life extremely complicated. It was driven by a fear of being forced to acknowledge that since puberty his body had changed from that of a boy to that of a man. Maintaining the fantasy that he was still a child kept the presence of the abusers at bay. Refusal to acknowledge that he was now a man, and had a man's body, meant that the rigid distinction between adult and child, abuser and victim, perpetrator and abused, was maintained. The risk of catching sight of his body, of what might be seen there, and the fear of what that recognition would do to him, to his sanity, was very disturbing. But he also knew that this defence was time limited and in order to find release from this tight regime he needed to face his own naked body in a mirror.

This was the first time he'd clearly articulated this dilemma. It was apparent to both of us that, having braved the ritual of circumcision, this was the next challenge. Undressing became the central focus of much of our remaining time together and at one point was to threaten not only the continuation of his therapy and its success, but also my own professional reputation.

* * *

The next step in this process of "moving in" to his new home would occupy us for the next year and a half. It was vitally important, he told me, that no one apart from the two of us knew of the existence of the bedsit, not even his sister. He began by making short visits to the area. He would arrive at the consulting room clutching notes taken on his latest reconnoitring, records of what he had seen and heard. He was most curious about his immediate neighbours. These were observations for us to ponder. Over many weeks I was given detailed descriptions of the street, the physical geography, the architecture of the building, what he had seen. His main preoccupations were working out how to enter and leave the building without being seen and how to make sure break-ins couldn't happen.

The area was just off a London high street, near a famous canal lined by markets and shops selling recycled clothes, leather jackets, jeans, vinyl records, gay porn and incense. This area was soon to become quite trendy, with fashionable shops and expensive restaurants, houses and flats afforded only by the wealthy. But at that time it was popular with punks, left-behind hippies and gay men in their uniforms of plaid shirts and Doc Martens, as well as devotees of the Lord Buddha and the Socialist Workers' Party. Abraham's bitter experience of being assaulted had left him vigilant and frightened to be alone in many parts of London; but here he was beginning to feel strangely relaxed and at home.

After months scouting out the neighbourhood, he was ready to enter the room itself and begin the process of securing it. Our sessions were devoted to detailed discussion and research into different makes of locks and entry phones. He had to be able to vet others coming and going without being seen or their knowing whether or not he was at home. He didn't want any surprises, and experience had taught him how devastating breaches of security could be. Until very recently, he had abdicated these powers to others, unable even to conceive of the possibility that they might be his right. He required the time to rethink old certainties, especially to consider that he might be more robust than he had been given to believe. He got irritated when I pointed this out but I took this to be a good sign. His irritation was not with me but with the emotionally frugal and restrictive regime that fear had demanded of him. After many more months of careful thought, turbulent discussions and practical decision making, he announced that he was prepared to give it a go, ready to take the next step and to move in.

* * *

By dint of many hours of listening, I am able to watch, in my mind's eye, as this next process unfolds. It is a bright room approximately nine metres square, a good size. As you enter the room, there is a galley kitchen off to the left, with an oven, hob, microwave and small fridge. The walls of the room are painted a pale yellow, the trim and the ceiling, white. It has two large

Venetian-blind-covered windows. Abraham has purchased the blinds after much discussion, as well as a few pieces of furniture. There's a single bed in one corner with a colourful African-patterned bedspread he bought at a local market stall on it. Beside this he's placed a leather chair and a small table and lamp. The floor is already carpeted in pale brown but he's thrown a bright orange and blue rug on top.

A small crucifix is hung over the bed and on the wall opposite there's a large framed portrait of Abraham's heroine, Barbra Streisand. Abraham is an ardent fan and has all her albums. Her songs will also provide the soundtrack to the drama that is about to unfold in this room. A large wardrobe dominates the wall opposite the bed. It has two doors, one opening on to a series of shelves and the other on to a rail for hanging clothes. The final object to be put in place is the full-length mirror, which he affixes to the inside of one of the wardrobe doors, in such a way that it can be concealed to prevent his being caught unawares and unexpectedly accosted by an image of himself there. The looking glass is highly provocative and must always be approached with extreme caution and appropriate preparation. It is to be the centre piece, the stage upon which he begins to practise undressing.

The overall effect of the room is touching. Preparing the room, the choosing and placing of each object, has taken well over a year of focused "work". It has been time well spent, a profound process, the creation of a place for him to begin to uncover for himself his own desires, his likes and dislikes. He has been discerning and thoughtful, each object saying something about who he is and what he wants to say about himself. The room he has created, as Virginia Woolf would have appreciated, is his own. He has yet to spend a single night there and I am still the only other person who knows of the existence of this space.

Chapter Eight

The Mirror

*"Feeling real… is finding a way to exist as oneself,
and to relate to objects as oneself, and to have a self
into which to retreat for relaxation."*
Donald Winnicott, *Playing and Reality*, 1971

UP TO NOW, ABUSE HAS CIRCUMSCRIBED most of the thoughts Abraham has about himself. He is still subject to random and unpredictably frightening memories, flashbacks and terrifying nightmares. One minute he's startled, the next ashamed, the next manic, the next full of self-loathing, the next envious, all variant effects of the abuse he suffered as a child. Setting up his room, affixing the mirror to the inside door of the wardrobe and preparing to undress is changing this dynamic.

Abraham is in a fighting mood. To date, it has been an unfair fight. He has known only loss, defeat and humiliation. But now he is beginning to get a taste for what it means to feel real. Feeling real, as Winnicott points out in the quote at the beginning of this chapter, is more than just existing. For the first time in his life, he is able to conceive of the possibility of feeling safe, relaxed and at home.

And now, for the very first time, Abraham undresses fully and looks at the naked body he sees in the mirror. It metes out harsh judgments. The reflection is hard, brutal and metallically cold. There is no comfort here, no tenderness; he feels very alone. He halts at this stage for weeks, susceptible to the flood of denunciations pouring mercilessly from the mirror, and quickly puts his clothes back on. He thinks that real men's bodies should be hard, powerful and well-formed, like men's thoughts about themselves. His looks soft, and weak. He feels exposed, sunken, frightened. "I'm overweight, my arms are skinny, my belly's soft and fat, I'm weak, unattractive, unlovable, pathetic. It's all hopeless! Maybe I should work out, make myself bigger, stronger, but that would mean going to a gym and being seen, having to undress and I can't do that." And yet he persists. Every evening after work, he makes his way to the bedsit, opens the wardrobe door and undresses. He feels very alone.

But he is not alone for long. He senses their presence, the watchman who forced Abraham to do things with his hands and mouth and the cousin who raped him. Abraham knows they are about, somewhere, watching him, waiting for him. He can hear their whispered taunts, all their threatening nevers: "It will never grow; you'll always be small and abnormal; you'll never be loved; you'll never be a man; you'll never kiss a girl; you'll always only want what we do to you; you'll never defeat us; we'll always have you; you'll never escape us; we are all you have, all you want."

For months the outcome is the same. He undresses tentatively, feels vulnerable and frightened, as if he is again a little boy left all alone with these men. He knows he mustn't give up or "they" will have won. He is both excited and repelled by what is reflected in the mirror. His gaze moves downward, slowly and deliberately. Each time he looks at his penis he sees the image of both a vulnerable little boy and a man. Standing there he is flooded with hateful thoughts, and again becomes the victim of memories, images, flashbacks of being grabbed, forced down, raped, triumphed over. Over the next months, the undressing becomes a battle between hope and fear; hoping he'll triumph over these men, force the shame out of himself and back into them, and fearing a re-enactment, here and now, in his room. His depression and anxiety intensify and I too am frightened. I fear I'll lose him, that he'll become unreachable, that he has taken on too much, that he'll be destroyed by this process. This daily ritual of undressing is accompanied by acute stress and other symptoms of trauma. He breaks out in heavy sweats, feels as if he's having a heart attack and is in imminent danger of dying. He hyperventilates and is overwhelmed by fear. The abusers are now regular inhabitants of his room. Abraham can smell them as he enters it. He is disturbed at being both excited and disgusted by their presence. For several months, the drama plays itself out to the same conclusion: he succumbs and fear takes over. He submits and engages in self-hating masturbation. Ejaculation intensifies his self-disgust.

The mirror has become a source of dread. He feels he is being laughed at, mocked, ridiculed by his own image, the weak, evil, perverted figure he sees. He doubts any contrary view I might have of him. He tells me that "the one you see, that's not the real me; that's me fooling you; you're a fool for believing that I'm good. Only I see the real me."

The New York psychoanalyst Michael Eigen once wrote that "everything is derived from the vicissitudes of love" (*The Psychotic Core*, 1986). We all need to "know" that someone holds us in mind. Isn't this what keeps us from falling out of being, from disappearing into despair? We can psychically and indeed physically die from lack of love. But when love and care aren't available, possession and control will fit the bill. Abraham longs to be seen and loved. In this regard, his family have disappointed him. As a small child he was left behind with his resentful aunt for whom he was simply a nuisance to be pushed away; he can still hear his mother's laughter as he is being raped in the bathroom not five feet away from her on the other side of the door. So, when anything is better than nothing, when the reality of hell is better than the nothingness of limbo, when the devil is better than no one, the attentions of the abuser fit the bill. Abraham often told me that he found it impossible to get them out of his mind, that he passionately hated them. He felt that he was constantly being watched, and was hallucinating them into his daily life, into both his day and night-time dreaming. This obsession is in operation as he continues to undress in front of his mirror.

I watch as he becomes increasingly depressed. His

arrival at the sessions becomes even more erratic; he's often very late, leaving only a few minutes for us to talk, and once in the room the old silences return. He despairs of anything ever changing and again tells me that he's failing in therapy, going backwards, maybe he should give up or stop for a while, take a break. I resist this with all my power but am also becoming increasingly concerned. He tells me that he sometimes has thoughts of suicide.

But he keeps showing up and sometimes that is enough. I'm reassured by his doggedness. I can see that he too is relieved to be back in my room, back with me. He has this place to return to, to tell me about his losses, his disappointments, his despair and even darker thoughts. During one session as he talks of suicide, he tells me that it's not about killing himself but wanting to do away with someone or something that is lodged inside him, of wanting to kill the "watchman", to eradicate the cousin's penis he can still, at times, feel inside him.

The approach he is taking with regards to undressing begins to remind me of how I imagine soldiers are trained. It is painful and at times humiliating but I can also see that he is building up stamina, flexibility and understanding. Undressing is becoming a practical training ground where difficult manoeuvres are rehearsed over and over again. The act of simply unbuttoning his shirt and looking at his bare chest in the mirror is hard work, but each time he does it, he gains a little more strength, builds up healthy muscle memory, and makes what was once impossible possible. What for most men is just an everyday act is for Abraham an act of great courage and hugely significant.

* * *

In one of the uncanny coincidences that often occurred during my time with Abraham, my Buddhist teacher, knowing nothing of my work as a therapist, one day suggested that I begin a practice that also entailed working with a mirror. In this practice the mirror is used, in combination with periods of intense meditation, to examine long-held thoughts and beliefs about the self. Projections are examined, challenged and questioned. The point of this practice, as I understood it, is to disrupt the very notion of a solid self. Normally we use a mirror to confirm the perceptions we have collected about ourselves over many years and honed into a set of beliefs and certainties that we then hold as our "true self". The mirror is like a piece of sticky fly-paper, trapping and binding us to our narcissism. But in this simple Buddhist practice, the mirror is used rather as a vehicle of deconstruction, freeing us to engage in curiosity and self-reflection, which in turn release us into a freer, more creative experience of self.

* * *

Over the many weeks and months of practising undressing, something slowly began to change. It was Abraham who first noticed it. He remarked that at times the mirror seemed to take on a different sheen, to reflect differently; the images it displayed were subtler, less certain, less defined. He spoke of the mirror's surface becoming moist and cloudy, as if steamed up by a shower. The image he encountered there, at times, disappeared as if into a haze. He spoke of feeling confused, of not knowing what was happening. I suggested that maybe this was a good thing, that what was becoming less rigid was not the image in the mirror but rather how he was beginning to view himself. I reminded him that he had been unable to undress for so long, for fear of catching sight of what he'd become, a man, a male body. Maybe now, he would be able to conceive of the possibility that not all men were bad and that the male body might not always be used as a weapon.

Chapter Nine

Undressing

*"All human selves are false selves – the linguistic clothing
that hides our essential emptiness."*
Phil Mollon, *Shame and Sexuality*, 2002

BY THIS TIME ABRAHAM HAD MOVED fully into his own
room. It had been a long and at times frightening process, taking over a year. He spent most evenings there
practising undressing. We had been meeting twice and
sometimes three times a week for over nine years. During that time, I had moved my consulting room twice.
Two years into Abraham's therapy, I'd left the safety
and anonymity of the convent grounds and moved into
a clinic near where I lived. The second move was far
more challenging, and I hesitated for some time before

I made it, as it was into a consulting room I'd set up in my own home. I also asked Abraham to begin to pay me. At the convent, the cost of therapy was covered by a charity and initially, when I was a trainee, I wasn't paid. But now I asked him what he could afford to pay. I had finished my first training and developed a private practice, and was making a living solely from my therapy work. He had recently received promotion and a pay rise at work and he figured he could afford twenty pounds a week. Other wealthier patients were paying me more, so I was happy to go with this. In our new surroundings, Abraham was also confronted by even more of me, the details of my life, my furniture, my pictures, my dog and the sounds of another person in the house, my partner. That he was now able to accommodate all this change suggested that we had pulled off something quite profound. No longer did he need me to be anonymous, no longer "the Christian family man". He could bear something more real, more genuine. And with all this came the dawning realisation that change doesn't always have to be traumatic, or for the worse.

* * *

It's a dull winter's evening. As usual, I have been working

since early morning and Abraham is my last patient. He arrives on time, takes his coat off, sits down, catches my gaze and holds it. Neither of us speak for a few minutes. Every aspect of his behaviour – the punctuality, the immediate and prolonged silence and the directness of his eye contact – gives me notice that he is about to take another leap. In the silence I feel both anticipation and discomfort; I have the distinct impression that I am about to be put through some test. Then, as if to confirm my suspicions, he leans forward in his chair and proclaims: "I need to undress here with you, in this room. I need you to see me naked."

The interchange that follows goes something like this:

Me: "What? You want to take your clothes off, here?"

Abraham: "Yes. Is that all right with you?"

Me: "I don't know, I'll have to think about it. What do you mean? I really don't know if that's a good idea. Anyway, why?"

He doesn't answer immediately but looks at me with a Buddha-like smile on his face, patient, affectionate, encouraging and wise. He tells me that I must be brave, find my courage, that he must undress, and that he needs me to be a witness to this. He follows this up by saying: "You know, I really trust you. And now you have to trust yourself."

His words throw me back to my sixteen-year-old self, having escaped the Catholic priests and arrived at the safe haven of the "Protestant school". My wonderfully wise English teacher, Mrs Leach, is telling me that I'll be OK, that I'm not stupid but bright, that I can learn and don't have to be so afraid, that I can trust my own mind. And just as suddenly I am struck by how much we both, Abraham and I, have changed over the years. The initially useful dynamic where one person plays the patient, the apprentice or student, and the other the therapist, master or teacher, has changed too, has become less one-sided. And just as parents must make way for the wisdom and maturity of their adult children, so must therapists. This change has been happening slowly and in subtle ways and of course I've learned to trust him! How could I not? Every move, every new ritual he's invented has arisen in his imagination as a need he has recognised in himself. My role has been to hold out for curiosity, to encourage him to recognise and face his fears, rather than direct the process.

And now what he tells me is that he needs to undress in my consulting room. I am feeling the weight of this new demand, this new need, both professionally and personally. It transgresses every norm and contravenes all psychotherapeutic protocol. I might even be risking my career. I could be struck off.

* * *

Abraham is a very literal man. He is adept at using symbols and metaphors, searching out images to more richly explain himself and his experience, but he also needs to find real solutions in the world. He possesses a practical hunger and eagerness for change. His solitary battles with the mirror have left him feeling exhausted and generally fed up with the compulsive and repetitive nature of his suffering. It was in thinking of how he could break this cycle that he came upon the idea that he needed to undress in front of me. When he first speaks of this, I mistakenly assume that he is making reference to a symbolic undressing. He cuts through my musings with a firm "No, not metaphor or symbolism. I need to undress, to strip, in this room, to be seen by you, see you looking at me." Finally, I get it. He needs to find out whether he can be naked in front of another man and survive. He's spent too long entrapped in strategies to avoid any situation that might threaten just such an encounter. He is unable to undress publicly, unable even to be thought of by another as undressed, or not fully buttoned and zipped up. Remaining totally covered at all times means that he can never enter a public toilet, including the toilets at work, never join a gym, learn to swim, have friends over, in case he needs to use the toilet. It means never going on holiday, avoiding any family event that might involve sleep overs, and it makes even the thought of a date, an encounter that might lead to sex, impossible, so no relationships, no marriage, no children, no love. The deprivation implicit in this regime is all encompassing, and he is sick of it. He feels confident that his proposal will be a good safe starting point.

But he has his own doubts too. He wonders if he is ready. Maybe he should wait, do some exercises at home, work out, try to build a bigger, better body first. By the following session, however, he's discounted this idea as totally missing the point, simply repeating an old pattern, defining himself by what he imagines, fears, hopes others, including me, might want from him. I too begin to wonder whether I'm having doubts about his undressing because I'm caught up in trying too hard to "be the proper therapist", hijacked by a need for safety and certainty. He urges me to have faith in him and in myself.

* * *

It is a cold day. He removes his old green anorak and puts it on the couch. He takes off his pullover, folds it, and with some tenderness carefully lays it next to his anorak. He sits back down on the chair and takes off his shoes and socks. I notice that one sock has a hole in the heel and that he is trying to hide this from me. He notices, sees my interest, and after the briefest of hesitations, smiles. "Not perfect." He stops there for some considerable time. Is he losing his nerve? I pray he won't. Then he begins to unbutton his striped dress shirt. He gazes down, removes the shirt and stands up. He is in a sleeveless undershirt. His arms are dark, very black, hairless, elegantly long. The shirt is folded, added to the growing pile on the couch, defensive emblems, like the shedding of some old skin.

Watching this, I feel shy; tears well up, I have to stifle a sob. He doesn't notice, I think. The whole scene is so tender; the clothes resting on the couch and his shoes, somewhat worn down, the backs broken where he's forced his feet into them, laces still tied, like a little boy in a hurry. I am struck by a new sharp sadness. The left-behind clothes, somehow especially those shoes, hold a kind of grief. He stops, looks at me. I hold his gaze. The moment expands. Time holds. There is a recognition, new to both of us, of an awareness that each of us is totally alone, vulnerable, uncertain, frightened and yet together engaged in something extraordinarily good, right and brave. He then takes a deep breath and pulls the vest over his head. This too he folds. He looks at me again, this time smiling, and tells me that he had considered buying some new underpants for this special occasion. But then he decided against it: "I needed you to see me as I am, normally. I need to see that you won't judge me, feel sorry for me, just see me." At this moment, after this admission, we simultaneously let out a loud sigh. A barrier falls and as if for the first time, we look at each other, without expectations, judgments or desires of any kind. It is just a moment, but I know that it will last for ever. At that moment, I know with absolute certainty that all will be well. That for this brief moment, he has broken free, and perhaps so have I.

He stops, takes a few deep breaths and begins to undo the belt of his trousers. He removes them, sagging from the day's wear, and unceremoniously adds these to the folded pile of clothes on the couch. Once more he hesitates, looks at me and then removes his underwear. He stands in front of me, naked. I see a shiver run through him. The scene puts me in mind of a young child emerging wet and shivery after bath-time. He sits down on the chair, looks at me and uncrosses his legs.

For some time we sit across from each other, silent, expectant. He is undressed, I am not, but somehow the nakedness and vulnerability are shared. Then there is a brief moment of self-consciousness but that too passes. We relax and he tells me about his weekend, about what happened that day at work.

* * *

After he leaves, I am left wondering whether he will want to repeat this in every subsequent session. Abraham's undressing forces me to acknowledge that I have entered a revolutionary profession. I realise that what we are engaged in is in no way eccentric, provocative or transgressive, but rather is exactly what we should be doing. In simple terms, I find that I am faithfully carrying on the work of a lineage of psychotherapists and psychoanalysts from Freud, Ferenczi, Lacan, Klein, Laing and Winnicott down to the present day. They found that working with others requires treading paths that are fraught with risks. And Abraham is the making of me as a psychoanalyst, forcing me to open myself up to the chaos, distress and darkness of his life, demanding that I feel, think, act and speak in ways that are radically fearless and dangerously intimate.

My main support and guide at this time is Barbara, my new supervisor. Years before, she had travelled to London from New Zealand to study with R.D. Laing, who was then at the vanguard of a new approach to psychiatry. It focused on respecting the words of the patient as opposed to seeing them as symptoms, confirmation of madness. Her clear-headedness and faith in both Abraham and me had the effect of enabling us to think and act with confidence and freedom and to find our way through a maze of old complications.

Chapter Ten

On Being Alone

*"I had never suspected that the key to my private
reality might lie in so apparently simple a skill as the
ability to let the senses roam unfettered by purposes.
I began to wonder whether eyes and ears might not
have a wisdom of their own."*
Marion Milner, *A Life of One's Own*,1934

ABRAHAM NEVER AGAIN UNDRESSED IN FRONT of me.
Once was enough. But where had this ceremonial
undressing landed him? It was as if something old and
toxic, a long-held certainty had been questioned. At the
start of the session immediately following the undressing, he said: "You saw my body, but not as I look at
my body. I could tell you weren't shocked, that what

you saw was normal, even though I don't see that. I say my body, but it isn't mine yet. I can and I can't feel it. I live inside it. But it isn't mine yet. It's all the thoughts I have about it, and me. I keep thinking about myself. It's there with all the judgments and thoughts I can't stop thinking. I tell you that I hate my body, but really it's the other way around: it hates me, it's ashamed of me."

In 1960, Donald Winnicott delivered an extraordinary paper at the University of London's Institute of Education with the unassuming title "Morals and Education", in which he refuted the idea that morals have to be taught to young children. In this lecture, he criticised religion for saying too much about original sin and nothing about original goodness. He argued that religion steals the natural goodness inherent in a child and turns it into its own artificial set of "morals". The goodness that religion steals from the child is then placed up in the sky and given the name of God.

This chimes with what the Tibetan gentleman said about "no struggle" in those strange and powerful teachings he gave years ago in Clapham. Since hearing him speak, I have often challenged the very different lessons that were drummed into me as a child. That early religious propaganda was not to be questioned then and at times still proves hard to shift. It is easy to believe that all the mess, the anger, resentment, jealousy, pettiness and meanness that I experience in myself come from a bad place, from original sin. But the experience of working with all my patients, with people like Abraham, and with my own mind in both therapy and meditation makes a nonsense of this view. The belief in original sin, which these days manifests in the guise of self-criticism, defensive narcissism and self-harming, is destructive of change itself. By contrast, the experience of "no struggle" or what the philosopher Philippa Foot has termed "natural goodness" allows one to unhook oneself, to free oneself and begin afresh. Discovering "no struggle" disrupts that irritating obsessive drive to get to the bottom of things and allows one to settle into curiosity and from there see, feel, hear and relax into the freshness of reality. The quote above from the psycho-analyst and writer Marion Milner's *A Life of One's Own* elegantly points to this discovery.

* * *

Abraham had undressed. Such a simple act and yet one so many years in the making. He had shown me his body and to his great surprise and relief the event was entirely free of trauma, in fact it was quite ordinary, intimate and touching. He had seen my tears and I had seen his; in that sense we were both naked. The relief and the exquisite joy of being an ordinary man with an ordinary body, able to feel good in himself, were now his to hold. Again following Winnicott, Abraham had regained a taste of the sanity and goodness that had been appropriated by "false gods", the men who had so violently abused him.

And yet however real a shift his undressing had proved to be, like any breakthrough, discovery or new insight, it was a slippery fish to hold on to. Old habits of self-harm and familiar, harshly critical voices would sometimes renew and reassert themselves. Deeply engrained by years of repetition, they easily glossed over new ways of seeing. It was not unusual for real insights to be quickly followed by a descent into despair and depression.

A few weeks after the undressing, Abraham tells me that he's been masturbating several times a day and is frightened he cannot control it. He compares the act itself to that of plunging a knife angrily and repeatedly into his genitals. When he undresses, his mind becomes flooded with "memories" of his disgrace and his disgracefulness. He is left feeling exhausted and terribly lonely, banished from the enviable world of all the easy-going relationships he sees around him. He fears that his cousin's curse about never being loved is coming true. He tells me about a young woman at work whom he would like to talk to, get to know, but says he can't approach her and fears rejection. There are also friends his sister brings back to her flat and introduces him to, but he finds he is barely able to utter a word. He is convinced that he is attractive only to gay men and he can't help but see them as weak and evil, committing shameful acts; that is, he sees them as men like him, perverted and sick. The masturbation fantasies are still solely focused on the two abusers, who hold him captive with thoughts of being wanted, a shameful object of their desire. They make him feel slightly less alone and momentarily alleviate a rising and crushing anxiety. Each time he masturbates, he hopes to find release, yet each time on coming, he is again thrust back into shameful loneliness. Each time he masturbates, the abusers emerge triumphant, reminding him, over and over again, just how trapped he is in this cycle of abuse.

Listening to him, I try to feed back what I think I'm hearing, that his distress lies not in the act of masturbation but in the accompanying storyline. I suggest that these are old and familiar stories, and although repetitious and with a never varying narrative, they remain utterly compelling. I add that I think that the compulsion lies in his attempt to return to the scene of the crime, but this time to triumph. "You seem to hope that each time there will be a different outcome and you'll be free? But fear seems to be visceral, a feeling you are more familiar with, the fear of failure." My comments do not seem to help much as every time he undresses it ends in masturbation and the experience shames and overwhelms him. He tells me that he masturbates in order not to feel.

This repetition plays itself out in the sessions. It seems to me that we've been dominated by this problem for months now, that we are quite stuck, at an impasse, as analysts say. Can't seem to find any words capable of disrupting this deadly repetition. Eventually, sick to the back teeth with months of talking about masturbation, I ask him – more out of boredom and frustration than anything else – if he might ever try to conceive of masturbation as being pleasurable. He turns on me in utter fury. The broken, small, anxious man has disappeared to be replaced by an indignant and rageful giant, screaming: "What a fucking idiot you are! You really are a fool! Have you heard nothing of what I've been saying?" He goes on like this for some minutes, yelling, blasting me with his fury. Then just as suddenly he stops. A momentary gap appears. We are held in it. And then for the first time in all our years together, at exactly the same moment, we both start to laugh, and soon we are dissolved in these tears of laughter. This becomes uncontrollable, and as soon as one of us tries to compose himself, to move on, it bubbles up again and we are again rendered helpless.

Later, when we are able to speak about what just happened, he says how good he feels, how much he loved laughing but especially seeing me so helpless with it. It becomes obvious to both of us that his outburst of anger was so shockingly full on that it shook us both out of anxiety. That which had oppressed us, kept us both careful, cowardly, disconnected and lonely, suddenly broke apart and we were free. It seemed like a sort of second, more spontaneous undressing and one that rendered us both naked. His sudden fury at me cut through my masochism, liberating me from feeling pity, that sickly sweet, poisonous form of hatred. Equally his rage freed him to really hate me, if only for a few seconds. We had made another fresh start.

The French psychoanalyst François Roustang wrote a book with the catchy title of *How to Make a Paranoid Laugh*. One of the many things I took from this brilliant book was that paranoia is the inescapable by-product of a cultish mentality. Cults, whatever form they take, fear and mistrust free thinking, and spontaneity. There are no jokes: cults aren't fun. Language becomes petrified. Cults solidify thought into dogma and empower the leader with omniscience.

The seduction of omniscience is an ever-present danger for psychotherapists too. When therapists take themselves too seriously, pose as all-knowing, wise and kindly helpers, they unwittingly become autocrats, ostensibly benevolent but secretly dictatorial. This stance in turn renders the patient the meek devotee, trying ever so hard to be good in order to be loved or cured. This dynamic might make therapists feel that they know what they're doing but it has the effect of disempowering the patient and often lands her right back in the dilemma that brought her to therapy in the first place.

The capacity to laugh at oneself, like the capacity to be alone, seems to be a primary marker of mental and emotional health. A few weeks after Abraham's undressing, I went on a three-month retreat in the high Rocky Mountains of Colorado. It had taken me years, after I'd so abruptly and furiously left the Catholic Church, to be able to connect with any of the wisdom I knew to be inherent in all religions. Having been so immersed from such an early age in the rituals and ways of one religion, the one I'd rejected, I had begun to feel a longing and a lack in my life for what they had addressed.

During the late 1980s and early 90s I, like so many others, had lost close friends to Aids. And while my partner and I were mercifully spared, and we had each other, I missed my circle of friends and was struggling to replace the ones I'd lost. I was without a community to belong to. Since meeting and being so profoundly moved and challenged by the love and wisdom of the "no-struggle" Buddhist teacher, I had continued to practise meditation. I can't say I enjoyed the practice but, doing my half an hour a day and the odd weekend retreat, I found that I was experiencing more space in my mind, and surprisingly that I was able to just do nothing, to allow my restless mind to relax, a feat of daring I'd never before been able to accomplish. Low-grade anxiety and guilt had always kept me jumping about, busy but not productive, and awareness of this restlessness was quite depressing and also made intimacy, especially with my partner, pretty difficult. So, I decided that if a weekend of sitting meditation made me feel a bit more relaxed and confident, I would see what three months would do. And as the retreat wasn't solitary – we were to be a group of about 150 practising and living together – I wondered how I'd cope.

The retreat consisted of three sessions of two-week duration when we practised intense meditation pretty well all day, and three two-week periods of study, socialising and shorter practice sessions. Meditation took place in a tent big enough to accommodate all of us and where during the first of the two sessions meals were taken in silence in Oryoki fashion, a highly ritualised Japanese Zen form of eating which is designed to cut one's neurotic relationship with food. During these practice sessions, the silence was gently but insistently enforced throughout the day. Alternately, during the study periods, we ate western style in a big tented dining area, had daily classes and, every few days, attended talks given by two exceptionally gifted teachers. Most importantly, we could talk our heads off during these periods.

What I found after the first month surprised me. As we completed the first study/socialising fortnight when we were free to talk, I found that I longed for the silence. I had felt an obligation to talk, socialise, especially say hello, nod greetings hundreds of times a day, and I was exhausted by this. Over the next two months, this pattern intensified. I felt anxious and jumpy during the study times and more relaxed and confident during the silent periods. In silence I also noticed more of everything, was delighted and moved by the perpetual, sometimes violent, sometimes tender, changes in the weather and the seasons. When we arrived it was snowing, and when we left it was once again starting to snow. In between it had been summer. A family of deer spent much of the day resting under the platform that provided the base for the tent I slept in. On the advice of a friend I'd bought a hummingbird feeder. I often felt joyous, often broken-hearted; I fell in love several times; I was at times lonely and other times intensely happy, and often both at the same time.

The period in retreat also showed how caught up I was in a neurotic search for confirmation. I recognised this old pattern as responsible not only for much of the anxiety I was presently suffering but also for having kept me shut down in childhood. A longing for reassuring expressions of acceptance and love from others continued to hook me and, in the process, alienated me from my own independence, adventurousness and basic intelligence. It also obstructed my capacity for intimacy and made me feel paranoid and unable to fully enjoy myself and others. In retreat there was no escape from watching oneself getting hooked by this craving over and over again. In sitting practice and even more during the study/socialising periods, I saw it everywhere. This awareness left me with no choice but to name it, acknowledge the feelings that I had for so long been blind and deaf to, and accept myself. Here was a primary source of a suffering that I had been bearing throughout most of my life. Gently working with it over those three months freed me up to feel both sadness and joy at the same time and released much hitherto untapped confidence. Those three months also helped me to notice the profound difference between "depression" and "sadness" and also between "loneliness" and "aloneness".

When I next met up with Abraham after three months away, he told me that he had missed me, but that my regular postcards had helped him not to feel totally cut off. And it soon became clear that he too had been hard at it, and that unsurprisingly, given how close we'd become and how much of our thinking was now strangely synchronised, his discoveries were not that different from mine. We had both been thinking about the difference between being alone and being lonely. "Maybe I've experienced loneliness as a punishment, a failing... something to be ashamed of. I punish myself when I feel lonely, I think it must be my fault, I push people away, I think I'm not good enough, and that if they get close they'll notice that there's something wrong with me. So, I fear people getting to know me." I suggested to Abraham that loneliness is a punishment dished out by oneself. He acknowledged this: "Yes, I feel unworthy of human company."

The next time we meet we talk about the difference between aloneness and loneliness again. Abraham tells me that for him, aloneness means freedom and loneliness is a punishment. "But I don't have much experience of aloneness because up to now when I'm on my own, I feel lonely and start blaming myself; I count all the reasons why people don't want to be near me, all the reasons I don't have any friends."

"So," I say in response, "if aloneness is freedom, then it must be the freedom not to need people to make you feel OK, or to feel so confident in their love and acceptance that you can enjoy the luxury of being alone."

"Yes, that's right. I missed you when you were away, but I was sure you'd come back, that you'd not left because you couldn't stand me any more, although that did cross my mind. I kept telling myself that you left for your own reasons, and when you finally came back, I was very happy to see you. It was scary initially, but then your first card made me feel that I am important to you. I was very moved, it made me cry; you just said that you missed me and that you were thinking of me. I really missed you at first, but it began to be OK. I still missed you but in a good way, especially when your postcards came every week. I began to trust that they'd keep coming. For a long time, I worried that they'd stop, but then one time the card was there and I realised I'd forgotten to expect it. I remember thinking that they were no longer a big deal and that I didn't need them any more. But I'm glad you kept sending them in any case." To this I said something like, "So, that must have been good, forgetting me, but knowing that I hadn't forgotten you?"

* * *

At some point soon after this discussion, Abraham tells me that he can't stop thinking about the number three. He sees threes everywhere; three friends chatting on the bus, a father, mother and a young daughter, three trees clumped together, three birds landing on the roof outside his bedsit, a man walking his three dogs.

Chapter Eleven

Imaginary Friends

"Human beings are essentially finders of substitutes."
Iris Murdoch, *A Fairly Honourable*
Defeat, 1970

IN A SESSION SHORTLY AFTER I returned from the retreat, Abraham sits down, is silent for a moment, then asks me: "Why have I never had a friend of my own?"

Intimacy between friends, even when one's life has been less complicated than Abraham's, is always a fine balance. In friendship there is the assumption of rights and privileges. Friends don't always respect each other's privacy. Sharing, the currency of friendship, comes laden with opinion, advice giving and "helpful suggestions", which are seldom dished out evenly or on a level playing field. Intimacy can be used to torture as well as to heal. Friendship opens one up to the threat of betrayal as well as to the joy of loving.

A profound change has taken place in Abraham. It has taken us over ten years of hard work to bring this about. One very simple way of characterising this change might be to say that he is now able to trust himself enough to cleave to another, to relax into and enjoy his first loving relationship. Therapy takes time and trust – these are the basis of change. It is a dish best cooked slowly. Abraham tells me I am his first friend; it is a special, a mutual friendship that allows him to speak freely. When we are together, he knows that what he says will be listened to, respected and go no further than the walls of the consulting room. We have together built up a common language, one not made entirely of words. We enjoy each other's sense of humour, are often able to read each other. I love his mind and his imaginative use of language, I am often surprised and delighted by him and look forward to our meetings. When we are apart, I often find myself thinking about him. He appears in my dreams. He knows that I care about him.

He has recently become aware of something different happening when he practises undressing. The shame has become less overwhelming, the process less traumatic, more tolerable. The repetitive, haunting images of, and thoughts about, abuse and abusers have become less insistent. It strikes us both that self-care is taking hold and beginning to overpower self-abuse. However, something I had said a few weeks before had prompted a shift in Abraham's thinking. I apparently asked him something like: "I wonder if you're caught in some kind of collusion. Are you colluding with the abuser's aggressiveness and selfishness? And as such are you betraying your younger self, the child who was left so catastrophically alone and uncared for?"

During our session, Abraham is once again in a radically creative mood. I have learned to recognise this state. I first witnessed the signs prior to the circumcision; then again just before he moved into his bedsit and began to practise undressing in order to challenge the tyrannical images in the mirror; then again when he announced he would undress in front of me. In this state he withdraws into a part of his mind that knows. He becomes quiet, thoughtful. The atmosphere is alive with potential. Here he is able, as it were, to plumb a clarity and a confidence that are usually not available to him, that seem to come from a place that has never been touched by abuse or by the violence and neglect he's suffered. He manifests spaciousness and solidity, a nobility that is completely natural and utterly sane and allows him to cut through old toxic identifications, to trust himself and to see with rugged certainty what he must do.

This is another magical phase in his therapy, a phase that is to mark the beginning of the end of our time together. The next time we meet, he rings the door-bell exactly on time, so I know that he is excited about something. He rushes into the room and blurts out: "I've seen them, it's them!" Apparently, a day or so after we'd last talked, he was in his room again practising taking off his clothes in front of his mirror and real-ised that he could hear a child crying. His gaze was wrenched away from the mirror, away, that is, from his own distress, and towards the sight of a group of chil-dren huddled in a dark corner of the room.

This is what I remember he tells me of his first encounter with the children, on that dark rainy evening in November: "I've seen them. The room was really dark. I had just started to undress when I heard a child's cry. When I investigated there were three of them huddled together and all of them looked terri-fied. I know what you're thinking. You think I've finally gone completely crazy. But that isn't it. I need strong images; I visualise in order to make things real. And they are real to me, at least they're beginning to be. I need them back. I'd lost them; they were stolen from me by the men who abused me. I want them back and they need me. That's what you told me and now they've made contact with me."

Many children have imaginary friends. They are useful and their manifestation seems to help with what is often a difficult transition towards shared intimacy. In these friendships there is no risk of betrayal and therefore children are free to experiment with their own power to hurt, control, punish and reward, to love and hate. Abraham has never spoken of having had an imaginary friend, so my assumption has been that even this helpful and rather innocent aid had been denied him.

But now here they are: he goes on to describe his imaginary friends. The first child is a very small boy, really a toddler. He is dressed in a brightly coloured shirt of some complicated and colourful design, probably African, knee-length shorts and a pair of tiny rubber sandals. It is this child who was crying as the other two tried to comfort him. Tears and snot stream down his face. The next youngest is a boy of about seven or eight, dressed in school uniform; he also wears knee-length grey trousers, a white shirt imperfectly buttoned, a tie loosened about the collar and a pair of scuffed Oxford shoes with grey socks, meant to reach to his knees but which have crumpled in a heap atop his unlaced shoes. Then there is a slightly older boy, a teenager also dressed in a school uniform, this time distinctly English. He stands between the other two, holding on tightly to their hands, and looks directly at Abraham. He seems to be completely overwhelmed by the distress of the younger boys. His impatience is palpable; he pleads with Abraham to help in caring for his young charges.

At the start of the following session, Abraham again bounds into the room and pounces on me with an urgent demand. "I need your help. I'm having a lot of trouble getting close to the children, especially the teenager." I must look baffled but manage to respond with: "So we'd better start with the teenager then, but maybe you can tell me a bit more about them. Who are they and what do they want?"

"They're the ones who appeared the other night in my room. They came closer, I recognised them, and also, I'm beginning to understand what they want from me. They want me to look after them, but they don't trust me yet, and I don't think I can care for them, unless you help me. They want me to keep them safe;

they're frightened and very unhappy. I'm most worried about the teenager. He never says a word and he's not at all pleased to see me. I don't think I'm very good with children, especially teenagers. They scare me. I think he'll find it hardest to trust me but without him I'll never get close to the others."

Abraham halts there, thinks for a moment and then says, with a look of concern: "The abuse done to the other two was more terrible but he was bullied at school, and after Sofia left there was no one to talk to and nowhere to hide. I didn't have a home then. Just that place I stayed, with the other children. I didn't have any friends. I was always scared. I wet the bed almost every night. The staff were kind, but it was too late. I couldn't let anyone, no matter how nice, get to know me. The bullying at school hurt me really badly. It's when I started hiding, when I stopped being able to pee. I felt so vulnerable. I was also so angry I was afraid I could kill someone. I wanted to kill them all, especially the boys who made fun of me. They laughed at me, at my small penis. They called me 'gay boy' all the time, even in class. That's why I'm always late. I was always late for class, never went in until the teacher was there. If the teacher wasn't there, they'd start chanting: 'Gay boy, queer, sicko.' They'd throw things at me. I always had to check my blazer, that they hadn't stuck something on the back while I wasn't looking. They hated me so much. I would always run away and hide whenever it was PE class. That was the worst, then the PE teacher would join in calling me names, laughing at me, make me do sit-ups, or run around the track, and they'd all make fun of me. I'd get punished for hiding and running away but I didn't care. I think I completely gave up. I'm surprised I didn't kill myself. I wanted to disappear so badly. I learned to shut down completely, to hide. I found that hating myself, especially my body, somehow made me feel better. It made me feel less frightened of everybody, of myself. I became certain that I was sick, disgusting, that I was a pervert with something bad inside me; I even became sort of proud of it. I agreed with them. That made me feel powerful. Hating everyone, myself and all of them, really helped me to survive."

Abraham wonders if he should ask the teenager to bring the other two children along to meet me. I say I think that probably he should just bring the teenager as he's the one who is most burdened, most responsible, and the one who is most in need: "It would be good for you and me to just get to know him on his own." And so it happened that over the next couple of weeks the "three" of us met together in the room. Abraham's latest preoccupation, the one about the number three and threesomes, was making itself known.

Chapter Twelve

The Teenager

"The essence of morality is '… making a willing suspen-
sion of disbelief in the selfhood of somebody else'."
Lionel Trilling, *Beyond Culture*, 1965

LIONEL TRILLING, THE LITERARY CRITIC, POINTS out in
this quote that immorality, human evil in all its forms,
stems from the failure to believe in the selfhood of others. It is possible to inflict the most appalling hurt upon
others, to torture, rape, kidnap, abuse and kill, and to
feel nothing, by the simple act of considering somebody else as "other". As he makes clear, "disbelieving
in the selfhood of somebody else", be they somebody
of another race, another tribe, the inhabitants of other
countries, of another gender or sexual orientation or

even children, gives licence to evil and throws morality out the window.

The abused child identifies with their abuser. Leonard Shengold in his book *Soul Murder* writes that this renders the child frantic because they have lost their sense of a "me" from which to orient themselves. They are flooded with emotion, confused and overwhelmed and possessed by the spectre of their abuser. Abraham was for many years unable to find any clear blue water between himself and the men who abused him. What they inflicted upon him had the effect of hollowing him out and filling that emptiness with themselves. Abuse is theft. Abraham's mind and body were kidnapped. But his soul was not murdered. Throughout everything, he managed to keep a bit of himself alive and safely wrapped up. The various rituals he invented for himself, the circumcision, the making of a room of his own, the placement of the mirror and the undressing practice he embarked upon, as well as most recently undressing in front of me, were each steps carrying him out of traumatic darkness and more fully into life. He was seeing things in a new light.

In his private take on things, it was his teenage self who had been left most implicated and damaged. Research and common sense tell us that symptoms of trauma become prominent from adolescence on. Current understanding is that adolescents begin to take on board that they aren't wholly dependent upon and therefore subject to adults, even those adults who have been inflicting the abuse or neglect. Until then the child has been forced to live on their wits, in constant "fight-and-flight" mode, perpetually on the look-out for danger signs. This heightened awareness offers the child a sense – no matter how illusory – of self-protection. However, when they are no longer a child and when the actual abuser has less power over them, the hyper-vigilance often increases. This is when the symptoms of post-traumatic stress, the re-experiencing, the hyper-arousal, the phobias, hiding, emotional numbing and self-harming behaviours begin to emerge.

From my work in this area, I suspect that at this point the young adult becomes fully aware that they have never been recognised as a separate individual. It is not simply a failure to have been seen, although that too is distressing, indeed it's the realisation that you have been seen, you have been selected, but not for your inherent value, not for you. You have been picked out as special only to be discarded, tossed away as something dirty, useless, a bit of old rubbish. This realisation is devastating. It can strip the young person of any last remnant of self-worth; it is a blow that knocks them off their feet and renders them unable to pick themselves up off the ground. There is a frantic need to obliterate, to blot out the insistent thought that you have no value beyond the use to which you have been put by those who have abused you – hence the self-harming, the alcoholism and drug abuse, the eating and cutting disorders.

* * *

Abraham arrives at our next session on time. We both take our usual seats and I wait for him to start. I can tell he has something on his mind. "You know he doesn't trust you either…" I get it immediately. We're not alone. There are three of us in the room. Abraham, as promised, has brought along the teenager.

"Yes," he says, "this boy is always listless. He doesn't feel safe with you, or with me. He's the one who's always late. It was hard getting him here today. He's still raw, he hates his body…When I look at him, I feel ashamed of myself. I've been so angry with him; I've hated him. But I have learned enough here not to hit him or attack myself. I realise now that he is very frightened of my anger, my impatience. And that's why, up to now, I've always kept him away… I've felt a lot of anger with him, shame and frustration…"

In the long silence that follows this confession, I find myself overwhelmed by two memories from school, not the terrible Catholic schools I attended as a child, but the one I taught at for eight years, just south of London. For a long time these memories have both been the source of feelings of deep shame for me. The first is of an occasion when, just after school had been let out for the day and I was trying to finish up some marking, a lad of about fifteen came into the room. He looked frightened and told me that a gang of boys were waiting outside the school gates. He knew they were going to attack him. He'd come to me for help but I was completely at a loss as to what to do. I suggested he just wait in the room, hoping they'd get bored and move on. He sat down but after a few minutes he told me he thought he'd go. I asked him if he was sure, and he said that he might as well take his punishment now, that they'd eventually get him. To my everlasting shame, I simply let him go. A quarter of an hour later, he was back and he had been badly hurt. I called his parents to come and pick him up and once again he was waiting in my classroom, but now he was silent and there was no denying what had taken place between us. I had betrayed him. These many years later, I am still haunted by the look in his eyes. My cowardice at not confronting the boys myself, but letting him go out there alone, was shameful.

The second memory is of an event that happened a couple of weeks prior to this. I had been spotted at a gay pride march by a number of boys who had gone up to Central London for what they termed "a spot of gay-bashing". When I arrived at work the following Monday morning, the walls of the school were festooned with graffiti, naming and outing me in highly explicit pictures and words. In the classroom, something disgusting had been placed in my desk drawer and that evening I found my car also covered in graffiti. Some kind colleagues and students supported me but, from the school authorities, not a word. Nor to my knowledge were any of those responsible disciplined. The caretaker painted over the graffiti but everyone had seen what lay beneath. It seemed to me that the message given out was that I had done something shameful simply by publicly declaring my sexuality, that I was an embarrassment, at best to be pitied, but not respected or stood up for. Throughout the next few weeks I felt on fire with shame and rage.

* * *

Abraham breaks into my reverie by saying that he's been

thinking about homosexual men, "not the way I used to, not angry, hating myself and them… I find I can think about men's bodies, compare them, the gay ones too, not only the size of their penises. It's funny, I find the gay ones seem freer, and I feel freer too with them; I can imagine undressing in front of them, frightened but not only…"

I respond by saying: "You used to be really worried and frightened by anything gay, by gay men. I remember you once told me you wanted to kill them. I wonder what's changed?" He tells me it surprises him too, but then says that "change seems to come these days… it comes from being with the children, with this one especially. I have to show him that I'm not scared. I have to act as if I'm normal, even though I'm afraid myself. I can't show him that. You know right now I can tell he wants me to stop talking, to run away and hide. But he's – no it's me – I'm not going to. He's now become like a very small child. He's very frightened. I have to be kind to him. He really needs me."

I ask him if he thinks he can do that – can he love him? His answer, after a few minutes of silence, is strongly affirmative. "I can; I know he will trust me. If you can accept me with all my faults and my weirdness, then I can love this boy."

Abraham goes on to say that for many years he knew he needed to undress but that it was the teenager who held him back. "He was frightened of homosexuals and that made him angry. I was afraid that what those boys were saying about me was true, that I was gay, and that being gay meant they thought I wanted to be abused, that I wanted to be raped. I hated them, hated myself especially: I couldn't tell the difference."

The teenager is the one who needed the anorak to keep himself hidden, "but not now. He's learning to trust me like I did you back then. He's still not sure if I can handle him. I have to learn to trust him too. He can be as negative with me as I am with him. He's smiling now… a couple of times at home he's put his arms around me, he cuddles me. If I've had a bad day, he sings to me … he sings very well." I'm surprised by this and ask how the teenager is coping with being here, being in this room with the two of us. Abraham's response is startling in its tenderness: "He feels despair and I feel hope. He cares for me, he's also my big brother… He's concerned for me. I sometimes ask him to put his arms around me… He does care, and wants to protect me."

I point out that he's twice used the expression: "he puts his arms around me". I tell him that I think that this simple phrase seems to sum up the vast territory that he has travelled in the years that we have been working together. "Like all of us, you are both adult and child, carer and in need of care, strong and vulnerable, protector and in need of protection." I suggest that putting his arms around himself is a gesture of love, of the loving care he's now able to extend towards himself, and that this is a very profound achievement and one that gives him a strong base upon which to care for and love others. Abraham starts to cry. Through his tears he manages to say: "I feel so sad but also so happy, but I can feel now, and I know they're my own feelings."

Chapter Thirteen

The Children

"Children tell little more than animals, for what comes to them they accept as eternally established. Also, badly treated children have a clear notion of what they are likely to get if they betray the secrets of the prison-house before they are clear of it."
Rudyard Kipling, *Something of Myself*, 1937

THERAPISTS ARE GENERALLY NOT GOOD AT blowing their own trumpets and this is right and proper. What happens in successful therapy is a mysterious and subtle process and most importantly, the work of a couple, not an individual. The reason Abraham and I met all those years ago was entirely due to what I've come to call Agnes's hunch, a supervisor's intuition that he and I might just hit it off. What tipped her off to this possibility? Whatever the combination of insight and chance, she was right. What began in me as anxious concern and in him as fear and suspicion grew into curiosity and matured into what can only be called love. I have never had children myself. But I have been a father, albeit a substitute father, an uncle figure to many of my patients.

Iris Murdoch once wrote of the need for aunts, confidantes devoid of the burden of parental responsibility, hope or ambition. Sometimes a companionable sister can provide sufficient love to bind siblings together through years of parental absence, neglect or sheer callousness. This was true for the young Rudyard Kipling, who spent the first years of his life with his parents, in the bright warmth of India, watched over by lovingly attentive ayahs. But upon reaching an age when Edwardian children were sent back to be schooled in England, he and his sister Alice were thrown into an alien and hostile environment. His parents arranged for them to board with a woman who, unbeknownst to them, was a vicious and vindictive sadist. Rudyard soon found himself the focus of her perverse attentions. There was no escaping her, and for the remaining years of his young childhood he was subject, as he recalls in his memoir, to "the secrets of the prison-house". Mercifully, he shared this predicament with Alice, or Trix. Together they were able to recall and therefore to hold onto memories of a loving home, of being loved.

Abraham had a similar experience. From the time they arrived as child exiles in the UK, he and his sister Sofia were seldom apart. When we first met, they were still sleeping in the same bed, two lost children finding warmth and safety in each other's presence. Although Abraham never told his sister of the abuse he'd suffered, the bond between them was formidable, as was the experience of being there for each other throughout the years when their parents were absent. Sofia was to die quite young, shortly after Abraham finished therapy. The fact that he was able to survive this terrible loss speaks of the strength he had discovered in himself, as Donald Winnicott put it, to keep wanting more of life right up to the end.

* * *

When Abraham's father had brought him and his sister to the UK, his mother had opted to return home, explaining that she wished to try to prevent the new regime from seizing her property. Nothing more was heard from her and it was assumed that she, like many others associated with the ousted regime, including Abraham's uncle, had been executed or was serving a long prison sentence.

But then, almost twenty years later, without warning, Abraham received a phone call from her. She was alive and well and living freely in the capital. When he asked her why she hadn't sent them word, reassuring them of her safety, she told him only that it had all been very difficult. He asked if she'd been harmed and she replied that she'd lost some of her property and was short of money but was otherwise fine. No further explanations were forthcoming. Then she announced that she wanted to come to London to see Abraham and his sister, that they were to get her a visa and send her money for the cost of the flight. She did not ask him how he or his sister were, or how they'd coped in the years since she'd last seen them.

As he told me this, I could feel myself becoming increasingly outraged by this woman's behaviour. It seemed clear, to me anyway, that she had abandoned Abraham and his sister, packed them off to London, effectively leaving them to fend for themselves. I suspected that she had just wanted to be shot of her ineffectual husband and when the revolution broke out, she had seized her chance for freedom. What was particularly disturbing was that she'd not bothered to let her children know even that she was alive, adding hugely to their distress.

And now here she was! Her children had apparently ceased to be burdens and were now assets with British passports, jobs and flats in London. It looked very much as if she intended to cash in. I imagined that she'd somehow got word of the change in their status and that this had prompted the phone call. But I didn't voice any of these suspicions to Abraham. I did not want to influence his thinking or deprive him of his right to work out for himself how he felt. I figured he'd suffered quite enough grief and deprivation without my adding to it.

Unsurprisingly, over the next few weeks, his mother's imminent arrival dominated our sessions. Abraham was thrown into a panic. He was not entirely pleased to have heard from her. What was uppermost in his mind was her demand for money. He experienced her request as choice-less, as a command. This terrified him and threw him back into the passivity of victimhood. He and his sister would have to go into debt to pay for the flight and the visa; and he feared – accurately as it turned out – that this was just the beginning of what would be an endless demand for money, money neither of them had. He feared he'd be black-mailed by someone who refused to take "No" for an answer. He was particularly anxious that he could lose the independence and freedom that his bedsit had given him. He was worried that his mother would see it as her right to stay there herself, would evict him and send him off to live with his sister or his father. He was unable to figure out how he could possibly protect himself against this occupation. An additional dread was that she would see it as her maternal right to comment upon and meddle in his life, and demand to know why he wasn't married. I too was alarmed for him and feared she would impede or even undo all the progress he'd made in therapy.

Panic, wrote Lacan, is the inability to express anger in the face of disappointment. When I repeated this well-known formula to Abraham, he became thoughtful. I could see I'd struck home. He looked confused, then angry and then just as suddenly he laughed out loud and said: "Sentences have always imprisoned me but that one is having the opposite effect. Of course, I'm disappointed and angry but not until this moment did I put the two together. I'm disappointed and angry with her. I've always thought that *I* was the disappointment, that I was the one who disappointed *her*. But in fact, she's disappointed me, she's been a useless mother and that's hurt me and my sister and now she expects us to just pay up, to look after her. That makes me really angry, but that feels good. Why shouldn't I be angry!?"

This drama arose at the same time as, and mirrored, the work he was engaged in with his own "children" in therapy, the four- and eight-year-old boys who materialised in his room. The children who had been trapped and stunted by lack of care and the trauma they'd each suffered. It is impossible to unpack all the layers of meaning implicit in their appearance and how Abraham was to work with them. So, I am going to focus on just one interpretation which for me holds an honesty about what I witnessed over the ensuing months.

When Abraham's mother returned out of the blue, the picture of a good parent let down by her bad, guilty, shameful and inadequate child, was suddenly shattered. The hurt and disappointment concealed by this false but for a time necessary fantasy could no longer be contained. It was at this point that the children found their voices; they were released from a long and isolating incarceration and their rage emerged as a scream of fury. Abraham located this in his body. He was unable to sleep, felt anxious and panicky all of the time and in therapy reverted to behaving as he had done at the beginning. At home the self-abuse increased, his sphincter tightened and his difficulty in urinating increased. He missed sessions, arrived very late, was again silent or monosyllabic, and when he did speak, he dismissed or ridiculed the interpretation I offered. He attacked the bonds we'd forged and retreated into a self-protective cocoon.

I too felt insecure. I was frightened that he'd trash the work we'd done, that this time he really would cease coming to therapy. The word that kept resonating in my mind was "uncontainable" but I was unsure whether this applied to him or to me. My own panic and habitual self-criticism led me to assume that I was failing him, that I should be containing this explosion. Fortunately, perspective was regained through supervision, and Barbara was not at all flustered by this turn of events. She helped me to see that, just because Abraham's mood was wild and dangerous, it didn't mean it was wrong. Indeed, his rage was most appropriate, healthy, even. These children had been released from a long and gruelling prison sentence for a crime they hadn't committed. And as a result, Abraham had lost something utterly precious that he would never regain: his childhood and adolescence. And in addition, he must now face the stark reality that those guilty of the crimes for which he had been so unjustly punished were to get off scot free.

On realising this, I knew I must hold out for the goodness of the bond we had forged together. Abraham's children were raging and frightened and desperately needed loving care. So, the choice was simple: the force of their rage had to be directed somewhere safe and I was called upon to do what any good parent must do, to hold steady and withstand the torrent directed at me. I told him in no uncertain terms that he had to arrive on time, and that if he didn't, I would not see him. I also told him that what he was feeling was perfectly normal and right. But he had to bring it to our session, so we could give these feelings the proper attention and respect they required. This didn't immediately have the desired effect. He got up from the chair and stormed out of the room, slamming the door behind him. But two days later, when we were next due to meet, he arrived on time and told me that he felt stronger, more able to think.

When observing young children, what becomes apparent is the sheer force of the emotion released when they encounter "No!", even from good and loving parents. They need to come up against this "No!". It is what holds them together from the outside. There must be a containing parent to stand firm and not react when feelings bubble up. But when a parent is neither safe nor present, and terrible things happen, as they did with Abraham – when the world is devoid of a protective and watchful "No!" – then children are left to impose a "No" upon themselves. But this self-imposed regime is far from loving; rather it is viciously totalitarian, pedantically and vigilantly critical. A monstrous watcher is summoned up from inside the child whose sole remit is to keep everything in place, to make sure that nothing shows. And as with all living organisms in the face of an unbearable threat, the spirit of the child goes to ground; they begin to close in on themselves and hide, simply to survive.

* * *

The arrival of his mother at exactly the time that his children appeared in his room turned out to be unexpectedly helpful, if not instrumental. In order to be able to trust the bond we have forged, Abraham had been forced to suffer an enormous but necessary disappointment, to let go of the false hopes trapped within the image of a "loving mother". And when she arrived back in his life, the cracks in this fantasy became gaping. Instead of seeing her as a "good but absent mother" and himself as a "not good enough boy", she was "baby-mother", complicit in much of the abuse he's taken responsibility for, and he the over-responsible "frantically distressed child". Simply by being there, his mother held up a mirror to the old fantasy. And he found himself able to cope with this loss. He knew that he had on hand suitable substitutes, as Iris Murdoch would have it, in his sister Sofia and in me for his less than useful mother. It was these real-life examples of responsible care that he now used in parenting his own lost and frightened children.

* * *

Abraham and his sister did decide to take out loans to pay for their mother to come to London. But her return to their lives proved to be a bit of a non-event. The work he'd done in therapy seemed to hold him. He didn't collapse. The panic attacks ceased. She did, as he predicted, say that it would be the proper thing for a son to let her have his bedsit, but he was able to fend off this demand. He was learning not to be tricked into making poor choices, and that guilt and shame, far from directing us towards the good, can provide the impetus for criminality, as Dostoyevsky and Freud have shown us. In fact, Abraham refused to let his mother even see his room. She stayed with his sister and complained endlessly about her lack of comfort, and also about her children's selfishness. Neither Abraham nor his sister liked her much. Although he described her as a child, "a big, fat, selfish child", he went on to say "but she is still my mother". To the therapist in me, this was all becoming very familiar, helping patients work through feelings of guilt as they learn to fend off demands from inadequate parents.

* * *

At Christmas that year, along with a card signed with his love, Abraham brought me a gift, a copy of Alice Walker's *The Colour Purple*. He told me that he thought that it was time to cut down to once a week in preparation for ending therapy. He told me that he had just done a weekend workshop to help men who, like him, suffer from the phobia about peeing in public places, paruresis, which had both shamed and inhibited him since early adolescence. The course entailed group work in which the participants openly shared their experiences. They learned that they were not alone, and importantly, that the problem was fixable. Then, after downing a couple of litres of water, they headed over to a shopping centre, and practised using the public urinals. On their return, they talked about their fears, struggles and successes while out in the world. During the three-day course there were innumerable trips to the mall, to get used to doing something that had for so long been impossible. Soon the men learned new ways of thinking about themselves and their bodies. They faced old fears and shared much laughter. Their camaraderie coaxed even this stubborn habit into easing its grip. This initiative once again came entirely from Abraham himself; I had never even heard of this therapy. And in fact, his talking of the self-help group proved to be yet another gift for me. For I too had been suffering from this affliction, albeit in a less severe manifestation, since adolescence. And as for him, it was a source of considerable distress and shame for me. So following Abraham's lead, a few weeks after he completed his course, I too did the Shy Bladder weekend.

Chapter Fourteen

Conclusions

"I've thought enough about them!"

A.M.,1992

WE ARE APPROACHING THE END. ABRAHAM tells me that to continue therapy at this point could risk feeding the abusers: "After all they are the ones who did wrong. I've thought enough about them." He thinks he'd like to go to university, to fill his mind with new, more interesting thoughts. How endings make room for new beginnings, how sadness is very different from depression, that some pain is natural: these and other such reflections punctuate his thinking over the best part of the following year. He applies for a place to study international development at a prestigious university and to his delight and surprise is accepted. He tells me that he'll finish therapy in the late autumn, once he's settled into the new routines of being a student. As the day of our final meeting approaches, we focus on how far he's come over the past twelve and a bit years. He knows that there is still much left to do. He's not sure whether he's gay or straight or bisexual. We come to the conclusion that this exploration can be a private matter, one best left to him, as indeed it was for me. This strikes me as yet another clear sign that my job is done. He is indeed a changed man and firmly connected to life and the future.

At this final session we both have tears in our eyes, but sentiment doesn't dull his wit. He's on form once again and says he's grateful that, in all our time together, I never once tried to cure him. I am at first confused and a little taken aback by this. Then suddenly I get it. The first of our many stand-offs had happened years before. For weeks he'd been insisting that I decide whether he should go ahead with the circumcision. I didn't buckle under what at the time felt like an onslaught. I held my ground and insisted that he had to decide, not me. Exasperated, he exclaimed: "Don't you understand? I'm mentally ill, I can't make rational decisions! I can't know what's right." I responded that if indeed he thought he was mentally ill then he'd better find another therapist, one who can cure illnesses. I wasn't that guy and I didn't think he was sick. "I know you're frightened and uncertain, but those aren't symptoms of illness, they're just normal reactions given what you have been through." And it was for this "holding my ground" that he was most grateful. I hadn't deprived him of his right to suffer and yet to carry on, to go ahead with what he knew in his heart to be right.

* * *

Psychotherapy is a redemptive project. It involves the triumph of listening, patient curiosity and intimacy over fear, shame and prejudice. For me Abraham's story confirms this simple truth. An African man, not wholly unlike the black men who make up the majority population both in our prisons and mental institutions, was initially diagnosed as incurable, a hopeless case, psychotic and therefore "totally unsuitable for talking therapy". Fundamentally, what this damning phrase implies is that if someone is unable sufficiently to articulate – to the satisfaction of the clinician – what the problem is, that person is therefore deemed to be mad. Abraham didn't speak in whole sentences for many months when we first met. His anorak had to tell the story for him since he was too frightened and ashamed to speak. It would take many months to build up enough trust for him to be able to remove even that first layer and begin to tell his story.

During the time we spent together, the connection between vulnerability and attunement became very apparent. Vulnerability is the ground of attunement. As in the children's game of Blind Man's Bluff, if you can't accept that you are vulnerable, you cannot "see". When my gaze or enquiry was experienced as disingenuous or insufficiently open, Abraham froze. This happened especially early on. When I was able to rouse my own courage and cease pretending to know "what's what and what's not what", as a Tibetan friend so elegantly put it, he would open up and be freed to think new, less shameful thoughts about himself. I experienced this same dynamic in my own therapy. We relax when we're being listened to with intelligence and attention: then even hard-wired defences begin to break down, of their own accord.

* * *

Abraham now lives back in Africa, and when he returns to London we meet for coffee and a catch-up. He also occasionally phones me to ask my advice. A couple of years ago, he phoned to ask about an important decision he was about to make. He lives in a large flat in the capital city. A young woman keeps house for him, and she has a very young son. This boy had begun calling Abraham "Daddy". The child had never had a father, and so, as is often the way with children, he had adopted Abraham. He had become very attached to his new father and Abraham told me that he loved the boy like a son. At bedtime, it is Abraham who reads him stories and tucks him in. Abraham also pays for him to attend a good school and walks him there each morning and picks him up at the end of the school day. He and the child's mother go together to parents' evenings and Abraham attends sports days and football training. Recently, the boy had asked Abraham if he really was his father. This gave him the idea that he would like to formally adopt the child. He put this possibility to the child's mother and her response was simple and straightforward: she said that since the boy had already adopted him as his father, it was only right that he in turn adopt the boy as his son. On the phone with me, he asked: "Do I think I'll make a suitable father?" I simply said something like, of course I do, and what wonderful news. "You have a son and you're a father!"

It is now March 2018. It has been twenty-two years

since Abraham finished therapy with me. I'm sitting having tea with a friend after walking my border collie puppy, Max, in Brockwell Park. My phone buzzes. I glance at the screen. It reads: "Number unknown." Unusually, I answer it. It's Abraham. "Hi Jim, I had to phone and tell you the news. I've just had my first swimming lesson! And only you know what that means! And I got undressed at the pool, in the changing room. And I'm normal!"

We talk for a few minutes about how great this is. He tells me that he'd always wanted to learn to swim but that recently his son announced that he wants them to go swimming together. "So," he tells me, "I've had to pluck up my courage and go to the pool and ask for lessons and get undressed in the changing room." He says that he thought he would have a panic attack but, in the event, it was all pretty easy. Then he adds: "After all, I undressed in front of you and you didn't have a heart attack, so I figured, I'll just have to do that again. And so now I'm learning to swim."

Then he asks: "So how's our book coming on? I'm so glad you're writing it. It will help lots of people like me. I'm proof that things can change. And people sometimes don't know that. I didn't until we met." I tell him that I'm almost finished, coming to the end.

This book was written at Abraham's request. When he first asked me to do it, I replied that I'm not a writer, have never written a book, wouldn't know how to begin. I should have expected his response: "Well, you can learn, and I know you can do it." Throughout the writing process, I've asked him several times whether he'd like to see what I've written. I ask again now. Once again, he replies that he wants to wait until it's published. Then he adds: "Because I trust you. I trusted you when I totally mistrusted myself… and it was you who helped me to get to this place, where I do now trust myself, I even like myself. And I can go swimming. I know you'll tell the truth about me."

Afterword

Just before publication, in response to a Christmas greeting, I received an email from Abraham telling me of a momentous event that had happened to him recently. He was keen that it be included in the book, believing that it would give much hope to other adult victims of child abuse like himself. With Abraham's permission, I have extracted his words exactly as they arrived. It feels right to let him have the final say.

Dear Jim

I have been meaning to send you a Happy New Year email and finally got round to it today. Happy 2019 and I hope that the Christmas break went well.

Today I went to a family (larger family) get together and a skinny older person arrived. We both greeted each other and it was about ten minutes later as I was passing bread to some of the people there that I heard him identify himself as my abuser. Around 45 years have passed and that day that I initially longed for – happened. I remember how I thirst for this day so that I could stab him to death and how that had changed throughout the periods after counselling. Face to face and he did not even recognise me.

I moved away from the lounge as I considered how I felt, what I should do and how to react. It was him, I could see that the face had aged and that he was much shorter and thinner than I remember him but it was him. I remembered what I read yesterday night in the Bible – Luke 6, 37: "Judge not and you shall not be judged; condemn not, and you will not be condemned; forgive, and you will be forgiven; give, and it will be given to you; good measure, pressed down, shaken together, running over, will be put into your lap. For the measure you give will be the measure you get back".

I thought about the boy that grew up then and I thought about the lost boy that struggled to find himself and the wrongs that he had done to others, whilst in pain. I thought about my wonderful son growing up safely next to me now, and I thought

"I forgive you (to my abuser) and I forgive me!"
I prayed that God would give me the strength to
continue with this resolution. He did, and I decided
to not speak to him or to see him. I kept a low pro-
file – in terms of keeping away from the area he was
sitting in the lounge. I did not want to contemplate
what to say to him, when he recognised me or more
importantly was told whose son I was – I didn't
want to pretend everything was alright and I did
not want to injure him so I prayed that God would
not bring me face to face with him. And he did not!
I kissed some of my cousins and appreciated them
and told them how much I loved them – them!

I realise that I am blessed to have so many good
human beings around me and one of my cousins
bought cakes to celebrate my birthday (two too late
but still nice). I ate it and was grateful for the cele-
bration that was more fitting for you and me. I have
spent much of the night thinking about love and
kindness – two items lacking 45 years ago but in
abundant supply today and in my life now. I realise
how blessed I am and how grateful I am for the
journey that we took together. God bless you!

Acknowledgements

Over many years, Adam Phillips's brilliance, his trust and insightfulness, both awakened and sustained me, especially during the many times I lost my way or my nerve. The compassion and wisdom of supervisors Barbara Latham and Agnes Beguin guided the course of my work with Abraham. Chris Oakley, Kate Gilbert, David Schneider, Jonathan Lewis and Julien Diaz kindly read drafts and offered important encouragement. At Short Books, Aurea Carpenter and Helena Sutcliffe were a joy to work with. The combination of insight, skill and enthusiasm they brought to this project has proved to be invaluably liberating. Joanna Rosentall and Lucy Engleheart, as fellow members of our three-person writing group, helped, with intelligence and imagination, to bring this work to life. I owe much to both. Finally, it has only been with the enduring love, insight and literary know-how of my partner Peter Conradi that I have been able to find the words to tell this simple tale.